Third Edition

MEDIA PLANNING

A Practical Guide

Jim Surmanek

Printed on recyclable paper

NTC Business Books

a division of *NTC Publishing Group* • Lincolnwood, Illinois USA

Library of Congress Cataloging-in-Publication Data

Surmanek, Jim.
    Media planning : a practical guide / Jim Surmanek. —3rd ed.
        p.   cm.
    Includes index.
    ISBN 0-8442-3512-1 (paper)
        1. Advertising media planning—United States.   I. Title.
    HF5826.5.S86   1995
    659.1'11—dc20   95-18554
                                                                 CIP

Published by NTC Business Books, a division of NTC Publishing Group
4255 West Touhy Avenue
Lincolnwood (Chicago), Illinois 60646-1975, U.S.A.
Manufactured in the United States of America.

5 6 7 8 9 VP 0 9 8 7 6 5 4 3 2 1

To Paula

Contents

Introduction

Advertising media are dynamic and ever changing.

The entire spectrum of media outlets changes almost daily. There are constantly new magazines being published, new radio stations, and old radio stations that change their formats, new television programs, new ways to reach people within television. Media vehicles tend to follow people's lifestyle shifts in order to address consumers' needs effectively. To the extent that people change, so do the media.

Perhaps the most significant changes affecting the media landscape deal with the distribution and reception of television signals. Now in its early stages of development in terms of its affect on *viewing* TV, the technology currently being tested will eventually lead to an entirely new media environment. It will affect what people will be able to view and how they will view. The *what* has to do with the predicted plethora of entertainment/educational programming and information/data banks that will be at everyone's disposal. A term like the *information superhighway* is certainly not alien to the readers of this book. And this highway is fast becoming a reality. The *how* deals with terms like *video on demand, direct broadcast satellite, addressable* advertising, and *interactive communication.* What is happening now with technology and the consumer testing of technological application to TV viewing will totally re-shape the future of TV and quite probably the future of all major media forms.

In addition to changes in the media landscape, the marketplace for buying and selling advertising time and space also changes dramatically. The cost of advertising in television and radio fluctuates up and down depending on supply and demand. Commercial time in broadcast media is both limited and perishable. If demand is high, the sellers increase their advertising rates. But unsold inventory cannot be saved, and advertising costs can decrease if demand is low.

Regardless of how media change, or which new media forms enter the scene, astute advertisers will need to assess the positive and negative attributes of each media offering before deciding to place advertising in it. Qualitative and quantitative analyses must be conducted. The analyses will require a comprehension of today's tools (e.g., cost-per-thousand, reach/frequency, etc.) in order to wrestle with tomorrow's media decisions. And although this book generally concentrates on five major media forms (magazines, newspapers, out-of-home, radio, and television), the reader will find that the dynamics and definitions discussed for these media equally apply to just about all media forms.

Similarly, regardless of how marketing changes, such as the evolving move toward *integrated marketing,* advertisers will need to understand the role of media in the advertising process (e.g., the importance of defining objectives and strategies before any media decision is made).

Who should read this book? Anyone directly involved with media planning or media buying or the approval of media plans, buys, and budgets. Among others, this includes advertising, media, and marketing staff at the advertiser's company, advertising agency and independent media company personnel, and media salespeople. Additionally, anyone who aspires to be involved with media (such as students) should also read this book.

What skills do you need to get the most out of this book? Nothing more than an average facility with basic arithmetic. The higher math of algebra, algorithms, and the like is not necessary.

While *Media Planning* focuses on media *planning,* nearly all of its contents apply equally to media *buying.* All references in this book to *media planner* could equally state *media buyer.* Until the 1960s, the planning and buying functions were conducted by the same person; that person would construct a media plan (defining which media should be purchased) and, upon approval from the advertiser, buy the media. As media became more complex, planning and buying evolved to specialized disciplines. This was driven by the notion that no one person had the time to become deeply involved in, and fully learn, more than one discipline. And, as media became even more complex (due the growth of cable TV, the emergence of spot TV and national syndication, the introduction of niche magazines, an ever-growing supply of media research tools, etc.), even the specialty of buying grew to subspecialties: national TV buyer versus spot TV buyer, TV buyer versus radio buyer, and so on.

The move to specialization occurred during a generally healthy and growing economy. Advertisers and their media planning and buying agents could afford larger numbers of people to deal with the media process. If these specialized functions continue, or if there is a return to a planner/buyer role, the media professional should understand all there is to know about media planning.

Along with the move to specialization of the planning and buying functions came the growth of independent media planning and buying companies (a.k.a. *buying services*). Today, three types of companies perform media tasks: full-service advertising agencies (some of which have an independently defined media operation), an advertiser's in-house media operation, and the independent media company. Regardless of which entity plans or buys media for the advertiser, the media dynamics with which each must deal are identical. To avoid any confusion, and because (for the purposes of this book) it does not matter which type of company does the planning or buying, all references in this book to the *advertiser* could equally say *advertising agency* or *independent media planning and buying company.*

For all of the reasons previously stated, advertisers, media planners, media buyers, and anyone connected with or involved in advertising media decisions must have a high comfort level with both media dynamics and media plan development. A *media plan* should always be devised before any advertising media are purchased. If you don't know where you're going, chances are you'll never get there. The media plan is the road map leading to your final destination: the buy. The plan cannot be created without understanding how various media work—how they reach consumers, how many consumers, the pros and cons of each media form, how they are priced, and so forth— i.e., their *dynamics.*

This book will first present media dynamics—definitions of various popular media terms and how these terms fit into media planning analysis. The latter part of the book deals with media plan development—how a media plan is constructed and what you should consider in that construction. Interspersed are related topics with which the media planner should be familiar in order to plan effective advertising efforts.

The Glossary/Index is a handy reference defining the most common terms used in media planning, as well as referring the reader to the specific page where that term is discussed.

If the reader is relatively new to advertising media planning, or has had little involvement with media, he or she might best start at the beginning of the book (with basic definitions). If the reader is familiar with the many terms used in media planning, he or she would be better served by starting later, referring to the Glossary/Index when encountering an unfamiliar term.

1

Overview

Different media forms are used for different purposes. Generally no one specific medium can accomplish all the objectives of a media plan. More often than not, several media offer benefits that should be taken advantage of if the advertising budget and copy flexibility permit. The media planner and media buyer must have intimate knowledge of the dynamics of each medium to devise the proper media solution and purchase media in the most efficient and effective way.

The more popular mass media are compared on several general bases in Table 1.1. These comparisons are *general* and based on *average* use of each medium. When used for different purposes, each medium can produce different results.

The following criteria usually apply to many if not most advertising efforts:

- **Audience selectivity** is the medium's ability to deliver a tightly defined consumer segment with a minimum of wasted (non-targeted) delivery.

- **Reach potential** assesses the medium's ability to accumulate large numbers of people within its total audiences.

- **Speed of audience accumulation** gives a sense of how long it takes for the medium to accumulate its total audience.

- **Geographic flexibility** deals with the medium's flexibility to provide advertising in selected geographic areas.

- **Lead time to buy** addresses how far in advance you will need to make a media purchase before the advertising is delivered in the medium.

1

Table 1.1. General Characteristics of Major Media Forms

	Broadcast TV		Cable TV		Radio	
	National	Local	National	Local	National	Local
Audience selectivity	Good	Good	Good	Good	Good	Good
Reach potential	High	High	Low	Low	Average	Average
Speed of audience accumulation	Fast	Fast	Fast	Fast	Fast	Fast
Geographic flexibility	Poor	Good	Poor	Best	Poor	Good
Lead time needed to buy	Long	Shorter	Long	Shorter	Long	Shorter
Advertising exposure control	Mostly Yes	Mostly Yes	Mostly Yes	Mostly Yes	Yes	Yes
Location at time of exposure	Mostly at home	Mostly at home	Mostly at home	Mostly at home	Mostly out of home	Mostly out of home

- **Advertising exposure control** relates to the medium's ability to control when a consumer will see/hear the advertising in that medium. Some refer to this phenomenon as a medium's ability to be *intrusive*.

- **Location at time of exposure** relates to the consumer's physical location at the time the consumer is exposed to the medium.

These criteria stem from particular advertising needs. Certainly other criteria might also be important.

Cost or cost-efficiency is not referred to in the table because it's unrealistic to prepare a generalized chart showing costs. The cost of any medium can vary from very little to very much, depending on what is purchased and the extent of that purchase. Notwithstanding, whenever media forms are compared, cost and *cost-per-thousand* are usually important yardsticks.

Additionally, advertising *creativity* is not referred to in the table— neither in terms of buying the medium nor in terms of creating advertising for the medium. Every media salesperson, advertising copy-

Table 1.1. (Continued)

	Magazines (National)	Newspapers	Newspaper Magazines	Outdoor	Transit
Audience selectivity	Better	Good	Poor	Poor	Poor
Reach potential	Average	Low	Low	High	Average
Speed of audience accumulation	Slow	Fast	Fast	Slow	Slow
Geographic flexibility	Good	Good	Good	Best	Good
Lead time needed to buy	Long	Short	Long	Long	Long
Advertising exposure control	No	No	No	No	No
Location at time of exposure	Primarily in home; heavy out of home	In home and out of home	Primarily in home	Out of home	Out of home

writer, and art director will confirm that all media can be purchased in creative, nontraditional ways and that highly effective, creative advertising can be created. All media professionals agree that media planning and buying is part science (which relies heavily on quantitative judgments) and part art (which ascribes qualitative considerations to media decisions). Intrinsic in the art of media planning and buying is the planner's and buyer's creativity in devising media solutions.

The terms in Table 1.1 are media jargon, part of a specialized language describing the dynamics of advertising media planning. These terms and others are defined and discussed in subsequent sections. All are equally important and should be thoroughly understood by the media professional and by those indirectly involved in media decisions. Interrelated terms are presented in sequential order to help the reader better understand media dynamics. For example, *rating, HUT,* and *share,* though distinctly different terms, tend to be used in combination in media analysis.

2

Rating

A rating is the percentage of individuals or homes exposed to an advertising medium.

Rating is generally used for television and radio media, but it is gaining favor in analyses for all media forms. For example, magazine audience delivery can be referred to as *coverage,* which is identical in definition to rating. Out-of-home media refer to *showing,* which is equivalent to *gross rating points.* The following explanation of rating uses television for the examples shown, but the dynamic involved applies to all media.

Let's assume a total television household population (those owning a TV set) of five homes. Let's also assume that only three TV programs are on-air at a particular time (e.g., 9:00–9:30 P.M.).

Two of the five television homes are viewing Program A as shown in Exhibit 2.1. Program A's rating is therefore 40, or 2 divided by 5 (the percent sign is dropped). Program B has a rating of 20, as does Program C, because one of the five homes owning a TV set is viewing each of these programs.

The same dynamics apply to calculating a rating for people (as opposed to homes). If two people live in each of these five homes, the total population against which a rating is devised is ten. As shown in Table 2.1, one person in Home #1 is viewing Program A, while the other person is not viewing. Both people in Home #2 are viewing program B, and so on for the remaining homes. In total, one person is viewing Program A, producing a rating of 10 (1 ÷ into the total TV population of 10). Program B has a 30 rating, and Program C has a 20 rating.

Exhibit 2.1. Mechanics of a TV Rating

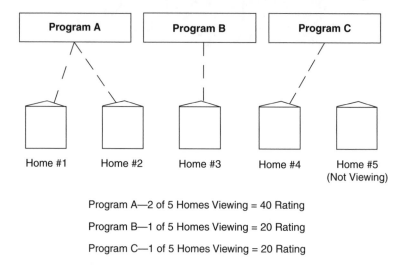

Program A—2 of 5 Homes Viewing = 40 Rating

Program B—1 of 5 Homes Viewing = 20 Rating

Program C—1 of 5 Homes Viewing = 20 Rating

Table 2.1. Number of People Viewing

	Program A	Program B	Program C	Not Viewing	Total
Home #1	1	—	—	1	2
Home #2	—	2	—	—	2
Home #3	—	1	—	1	2
Home #4	—	—	2	—	2
Home #5	—	—	—	2	2
Total	1	3	2	4	10
Rating	**10**	**30**	**20**		

Because ratings are percentages, knowing the population bases against which they are calculated is important. In the above examples, we used a universe of five homes and ten people. In Table 2.2 we demonstrate that the same rating applied to different population bases produces different *numbers of people* who are exposed to an advertising medium. As Table 2.2 points out, a 10 rating (i.e., 10%) for a

Table 2.2 Ratings Applied to Different Population Groups

	Program A	Program B	Program C
Geography	National	Market X	Market Y
Men population (in 1,000s)	90,000	900	500
Women population (in 1,000s)	100,000	1,000	600
Men rating	10	10	10
Women rating	8	8	8
Men delivery (in 1,000s)	9,000	90	50
Women delivery (in 1,000s)	8,000	80	48

national program, applied to a national population base, is equivalent to 9,000,000 men, while the same rating applied to a program airing in Market X is equivalent to 90,000 men. Bear in mind that what is shown as a program could equally apply to any medium.

Television and radio program providers, such as the four broadcast television networks and the many cable networks and radio networks, as well as their local market counterparts, use ratings to assess a program's popularity. If the rating for a program is high, the program will probably continue to be kept on-air. Conversely, if the rating is low, the program will more often than not be cancelled.

Rating is the most important broadcast term. Advertisers use ratings to buy television and radio programs, to determine how many people will be reached with their advertising messages, and to calculate how often these people will be exposed to their messages.

Program providers are also sellers of advertising time and as such also use ratings as one criterion for establishing prices for commercials. It's generally correct to say that the higher rated programs command higher prices.

HUT, PUT, and PUR

Homes Using TV (HUT)

Homes Using TV, or HUT, is the percentage of homes using television at a given time of day.

The first two homes in Exhibit 3.1 are viewing Program A; the next home is viewing Program B; and the next is viewing Program C. The fifth home is not using television at this time. Of the five TV homes, four are viewing. The HUT at this time is 80 percent.

We use television *homes* in this example. The same concept applies to *People* Using Television (PUT) and *People* Using Radio (PUR). The difference in terms derives from the population base.

Exhibit 3.1. Mechanics of HUT

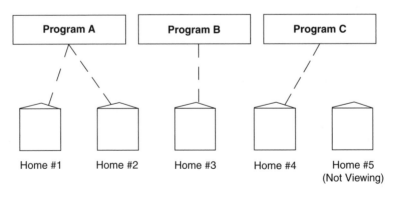

Home #1　　Home #2　　Home #3　　Home #4　　Home #5
(Not Viewing)

4 0ut 5 Homes Using Television = 80%

Although 80 percent of *homes* are using television in this example, the percentage of total *people* using television could be less. If we assume that two persons are in every home and only one is viewing television, the PUT would be 40 percent—4 people viewing divided by a population base of 10 people.

In all cases, the percentage refers to the available universe with a TV set or radio *in their home,* rather than to the total population. In the case of radio, the *in-the-home* aspect also encompasses *in the car.* HUT does not include exposure to TV outside the home, such as in a hotel room, on airplanes, etc.

Again referring to Exhibit 3.1, HUT can be derived by adding the individual ratings of all programs airing at a particular time as follows:

Program A	40 Rating
Program B	20 Rating
Program C	20 Rating

Total Ratings 80 = HUT

HUT levels vary by season, by time of day, by geographic area, and by market. The variations reflect work habits and lifestyle. Usage levels are lower in the morning when people are going to work. They are higher at night when people are home, but get lower as the evening wears on and people go to sleep. They are lower in warm weather, when people tend to stay outdoors more, and higher in cold weather.

Table 3.1 demonstrates typical variations in HUT levels according to eastern standard time (EST). Interestingly, because the Central region receives national television fare one hour earlier than the Eastern or Western regions, i.e., a program airing at 11 P.M. EST airs at 10 P.M. central standard time, HUT levels in the Central area tend to be higher than average.

People Using TV (PUT)

Like HUT levels, PUT levels also vary. The variation is different from one demographic group to another. Although Table 3.2 has been constructed based on a February rating report for Chicago, the overall pattern holds for most markets in most months, with the exception of time zone differences. As shown in the Table 3.2, PUT levels tend to be lowest in the morning, increase as the day wears on, and then decrease late at night. But the relative shift is different among groups. Note that teen PUTs drop dramatically at 10 P.M., while adult PUTs

Table 3.1. HUT Variations

By Season (8–11 P.M. EST)		By Time of Day	
Jan–Mar	64%	8–8:30 P.M.	56%
Apr–Jun	53%	8:30–9	58%
Jul–Sep	48%	9–9:30	59%
Oct–Dec	61%	9:30–10	59%
Annual average	57%	10–10:30	57%
		10:30–11	53%
		Average 8–11 P.M.	57%

By Geography (11 P.M.–1 A.M. EST)		By Market (11 P.M.–1 A.M. EST)	
Northeast	28%	New York	30%
Central	36%	Portland, Me.	11%
South	25%	Chicago	42%
West	22%	Des Moines	33%
National average	29%	Miami	21%
		Columbus, Ga.	18%
		Los Angeles	26%
		Reno	13%

Source: A. C. Nielsen.

Table 3.2. PUT Variations

Mon–Fri	Women 18+	Men 18+	Teens 12–17	Children 2–11
6–9 A.M.	13	8	6	5
9 A.M.–Noon	18	8	4	11
Noon–3 P.M.	22	10	5	7
3–5 P.M.	23	15	20	28
5–7 P.M.	37	31	29	36
7–10 P.M.	57	51	41	31
10–10:30 P.M.	55	48	23	8
10:30 P.M.–Midnight	32	27	12	4
Midnight–1 A.M.	12	10	3	2

generally hold; children PUT levels are higher than teen PUT levels at 5–7 P.M., but the reverse is true for 7–10 P.M. It is also interesting to note that women PUT levels are consistently higher than men PUT levels.

People Using Radio (PUR)

People Using Radio (PUR) levels also vary. Adult listening peaks in the 6–10 P.M. period; teen listening peaks in the 3–7 P.M. period. Through the year, listening levels are relatively flat for adults, but show marked fluctuations for teens, such as in the 10 A.M.–3 P.M. period during the summer (when school, in most parts of the country, is not in session).

The usage level of TV and radio complement each other: Radio listening is at its highest level when TV is at its lowest, and vice versa.

Table 3.3. PUR Variations by Time of Day

	% Men 18 +	% Women 18+	% Teens 12–17
6–10 A.M.	25	27	17
10 A.M.–3 P.M.	23	23	9
3–7 P.M.	21	19	21
7 P.M.–Midnight	12	10	18
Midnight–6 A.M.	4	3	3

Table 3.4. Index of Radio Listening Levels by Calendar Quarter

	6–10 A.M.	10 A.M.–3 P.M.	3–7 P.M.	7 P.M.–Midnight
Adults 18+	100	100	100	100
Jan–Mar	103	101	101	95
Apr–Jun	102	102	101	101
Jul–Sep	95	99	98	104
Oct–Dec	100	98	100	100
Teens 12–17	100	100	100	100
Jan–Mar	108	78	101	102
Apr–Jun	102	78	101	98
Jul–Sep	85	177	93	95
Oct–Dec	105	67	105	103

Source: Arbitron

Although the dynamics of the media terms are the same regardless of the population base referred to (homes, or men, or women, etc.), the absolute numbers can vary substantially. For example, Exhibit 3.2 shows that approximately 48 percent of women view television between 9 P.M. and 10 P.M. Compare this with Table 3.1, which shows a HUT level of 59. This difference is explained by the fact that other viewing population segments (men, for example) are causing additional *homes* to be counted as viewing households.

Let us assume five TV homes, each with four people (one man, one woman, one teenager, one child). As shown in Table 3.5, two people are viewing in Home #1, two in Home #2, and one each in Homes #3 and #4. No one is viewing in Home #5. In total, four of the five homes are viewing: an 80 HUT. The PUT levels, however, are lower and vary by population segment: 20 for men, 40 for women, 20 for teens, 40 for children, and 30 for all people on average.

Exhibit 3.2 Use Levels of Radio and Television
(% of women listening to radio/viewing television)

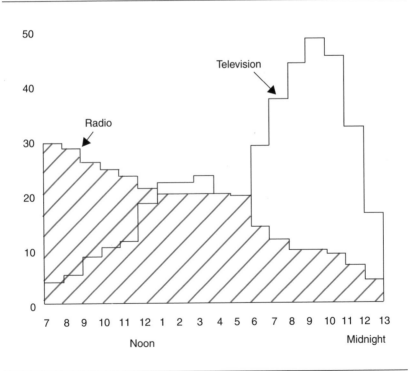

Source: Nielsen/Arbitron.

Table 3.5. Number of Viewers

	Men	Women	Teens	Children	Total
Home #1	1	1	–	–	2
Home #2	–	1	–	1	2
Home #3	–	–	1	–	1
Home #4	–	–	–	1	1
Home #5	–	–	–	–	–
Total	1	2	1	2	6
Pop. Base	5	5	5	5	20
PUT	20	40	20	40	30

Share

Share is the *percentage of HUT* tuned to a particular program. Because the dynamic of HUT is the same as PUT or PUR, the definition of *share* also applies to these terms.

In business, "market share" is used as a benchmark to express what percentage of the total industry sales dollars a company has for itself. Share in television is used in a similar fashion. It states what percentage a program, or station, has of the total viewing/listening audience.

Exhibit 4.1. Mechanics of Share

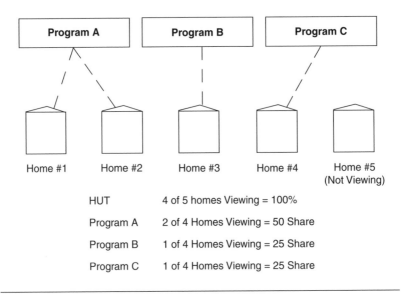

HUT	4 of 5 homes Viewing = 100%
Program A	2 of 4 Homes Viewing = 50 Share
Program B	1 of 4 Homes Viewing = 25 Share
Program C	1 of 4 Homes Viewing = 25 Share

Keep in mind that share is not projected to the total homes owning a TV or radio, but only to those homes (or people) viewing or listening at a particular time.

In Exhibit 4.1, Program A is viewed by two of the five TV homes available, but only four TV homes are viewing. Program A is therefore being viewed by 50 percent of the viewing audience and has a 50 share.

The share of a program in daytime might be the same as that of a program at night, but because so many more homes are viewing TV at night, the ratings of the programs are quite different—the ones at night have higher ratings.

Rating/HUT/Share

These three terms are interrelated. By knowing any two, we can calculate the third. As a formula, rating, share, and HUT can be expressed as follows:

$$HUT \times Share = Rating$$

Tying the three terms together in Exhibit 5.1, we see:

- 80 percent of the homes owning a TV set are viewing—80 percent HUT.

Exhibit 5.1. Interrelationship of Rating/HUT/Share

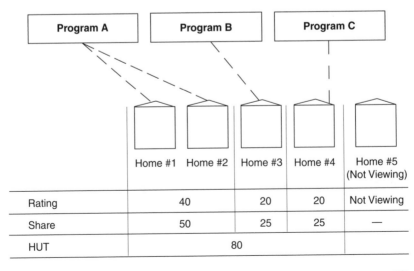

	Home #1	Home #2	Home #3	Home #4	Home #5 (Not Viewing)
Rating	40		20	20	Not Viewing
Share	50		25	25	—
HUT		80			

- Program A is viewed by two of the five homes—40 rating.

- Of the four TV homes viewing, two are viewing Program A—50 percent share.

Table 5.1 is designed to give the reader a sense of rating, HUT, and share across multiple demographics for the same programs. This table has been compiled for three reasons:

1. To reinforce how the three terms are interrelated;

2. To demonstrate why all three terms are independently important in any media analysis; and

3. To add to the definition of share by showing that the combined shares of all programs can be more or less than 100%.

Studying this information you will note:

- There is no direct relationship between a *homes* rating and a *people* rating. Program A, for example has the highest homes rating, but not the highest rating against all demographic groups.

- Ratings vary by demographic group. Program B, for example, has the highest rating against men, but one of the lowest ratings against teens.

- There is no direct relationship between HUT and PUT levels, although the higher the PUT levels for multiple demographics, generally the higher the HUT levels will be.

The HUT/PUT levels reported in syndicated audience studies do not necessarily represent the sum of the reported ratings. As shown, HUT levels can exceed total ratings. This is because *each TV set* in a household contributes to a Household Rating, but the home is counted only once for reporting HUT. PUT levels can be less than the sum of ratings. This is because other programs are being viewed, but none of these programs is viewed by a sufficient number of people to yield a statistically reliable rating (i.e., each is below the minimum reporting standards established by the research company).

Estimating a Rating

We can estimate, with some degree of accuracy, the share a program might receive. Just some of the variables considered are:

- Time period (when the show will air);

Table 5.1 Rating, HUT and Share

	Average Rating				
	Homes	Women 18+	Men 18+	Teens 12–17	Children 2–11
Rating					
Program A	25	20	15	10	5
Program B	20	15	20	5	5
Program C	10	10	5	*	5
Program D	10	5	5	5	*
Program E	50	5	*	5	*
Total HUT/PUT	70	55	45	25	15
Reported HUT/PUT	65	60	55	35	20
Share⁺					
Program A	38	33	27	29	25
Program B	31	25	36	14	25
Program C	15	17	9	–	25
Program D	15	8	9	14	–
Program E	8	8	–	14	–
Total	107 %	91 %	81 %	71 %	75 %
Other viewing	7	8	18	29	25

*Below minimum reporting standards.

⁺ Based on reported HUT/PUT.

- The competition the show will have on the other stations (Will the new program be opposite a top-rated program or a weak program?);

- Programs preceding and following the new program (A strong lead-in program is sometimes advantageous if we assume viewers will not change channels too readily);

- The type of program (Will it be a documentary or a situation comedy?); and

- The history of similar types of programs (Were they hits or misses?). We can also study the script, screen the pilot when available, and know the producer, director, and cast to determine if their talents have produced successes in the past.

If a new program is to air on Tuesdays between 9 and 9:30 P.M., we know that about 66 percent of the homes will be viewing TV. If we estimate the share of audience the program might receive—based on all of the above variables—we can estimate the rating of the program.

HUT	66%
Share	× 35%
Rating	23.1

The key word is *estimate*. It is a judgment calculated from imperfect data. Although it is based on extensive analysis of past performance, it is, nevertheless, only an estimate of what the media professional believes will happen.

A corollary to Murphy's Law might be "If anything can vary, it will." As we have seen, HUT varies by time of day and by season. Share varies for all the reasons previously stated. These differences result in rating variations—from airing to airing and from moment to moment while the program is on-air. Table 5.2 shows the rating received for two consecutive airings of the same program, and for each quarter hour within each airing. Even if the media planner or buyer had accurately estimated the average rating, the real audience varied substantially: from a high rating of 24.3 to a low of 18.4.

Ratings for Unreported Audience

The "population" referred to in Table 5.2 can be any population segment for which data is available from syndicated sources. One such source is Nielsen, which reports ratings for the demographic segments noted in Table 5.3.

Rating information can also be obtained for other population groups (for example, men 35–49), but there are two cautions involved. The first is that ratings, because they are a percent of a population base, cannot be added to or subtracted from each other. For example, one cannot take a 10 rating for men 18 to 34 and subtract it from a 15 rating for men 18 to 49 to determine a rating for men 35 to 49. To make this calculation, one must deal with the absolute population and audience numbers, and perform the following arithmetic:

- Multiply the reported rating for each audience segment by the population base for that segment to find the absolute audience.

- Subtract the audience of the smaller segment from the larger to determine the audience for the demographic segment with no reported rating.

Table 5.2. Household Ratings Fluctuation—Program A

Time	Week 1	Week 2	Average
8:00–8:15	20.2	18.4	19.3
8:15–8:30	22.8	19.8	21.3
8:30–8:45	24.3	23.6	24.0
8:45–9:00	24.3	23.6	24.0
Average	22.9	21.4	22.2

Table 5.3. Population Segments Reported by Nielsen

Age Cell	Persons	Women	Men
2+	•		
2–11	•		
6–11	•		
12–17	•		
12–24	•	•	
12–34	•		
18+	•	•	•
18–34	•	•	•
18–49	•	•	•
21–49	•		•
25–49		•	•
25–54	•	•	•
35+	•		
35–64	•		
50+	•		

- Divide the audience obtained by the population base of that unreported segment to produce an average rating.

The steps are illustrated in Table 5.4.

The second caution involves the "stability" of the resulting rating and the basic data being used to calculate the new rating. As will be discussed later, all rating information is based on the media consumption habits of a portion of the population and therefore can be affected by what happens in the *real* world.

Table 5.4. Calculating a Rating for an Unreported Audience

Audience Segment	Population Base	Reported Rating	Absolute Audience
18–49	1,000,000	15	150,000
18–34	400,000	10	40,000
35–49	600,000	—	110,000
	110,000 ÷ 600,000 = 18 rating		

Postanalysis

Buying commercials in programs that will air in the future requires predicting the future. The only way to know if the estimate is accurate (within the confines of available research) is to wait for the future to happen and have a published rating report for the period in question. This is called a *postanalysis*. For example, and using Table 5.2, the media buyer might have estimated in September that Program A *will* get a 22.0 rating during its November airing. The actual rating will be reported in the November ratings report (which is generally published late the following month). Further, because rating books report ratings for each quarter-hour segment (for many programs), and because a commercial will air in a specific quarter hour, the media buyer can also determine the program rating during the average quarter hour in which the commercial aired.

A postanalysis should be conducted for every media buy. Doing a *post:*

- Allows the buyer to better estimate for future buys.

- Gives the buyer information that can be used in future negotiations with TV or radio stations.

- Gives the advertiser a more accurate accounting of how much media delivery was actually delivered (as opposed to how much might be delivered).

6

Gross Rating Points/Target Rating Points

Gross rating points (GRPs) are the sum of the ratings delivered by a given list of media vehicles. Like ratings, GRPs are a percentage. Target rating points (TRPs) have exactly the same definition.

The reference to GRPs commonly indicates *household* rating points. This was the only reporting base when ratings research began. TRPs commonly refer to *people* rating points. As research companies began to produce ratings information for both homes and people, GRP evolved to TRP. Nonetheless, the terms are interchangeable so long as one cites which population base is being used in the reference. For example, it's more precise to state that a schedule is composed of 100 *household* GRPs, or 100 *Men 25–49* TRPs, than to simply state 100 GRPs or 100 TRPs.

GRPs offer a description of total audience delivery without regard to duplication or repeat exposure to the media vehicles, thus the word *gross*. Individuals, or homes, are counted as many times as they are exposed to the advertising.

To calculate GRPs, we multiply the rating of each announcement (or magazine insertion, etc.) by the number of times each announcement runs. If a program with a 20 rating is used twice, total GRPs are 40 (20 × 2). The schedule shown in Table 6.1, composed of 13 announcements across four programs, delivers 200 GRPs.

If a 20 rated program is seen by 20 percent of the households with a TV set, then two announcements scheduled in this program will be seen by the *equivalent* of 40 percent of households. The 13-announcement schedule shown, with 200 GRPs, will therefore be seen once by the *equivalent* of 200 percent of the population.

Table 6.1. Calculating Gross Rating Points

	Average Household Rating	Announcements in Schedule	GRPs
Program A	20	2	40
Program B	15	4	60
Program C	25	2	50
Program D	10	5	50
		13	200

GRPs are one way to express total gross audience delivery. Impressions, discussed in the next chapter, are another way to express gross delivery. In Chapter 8 on "Reach" we will investigate *net* media delivery.

7

Impressions

Impressions are the sum of all advertising exposures.

Impressions are the same as GRPs or TRPs, but are expressed in terms of *numbers* of individuals (or homes) rather than as a percentage.

Impressions can be calculated in one of two ways:

- Multiply the GRPs/TRPs delivered to a given population group by the number of people in the population group.

- Add the audience delivered (number) for each announcement (or magazine insertion, etc.) in a schedule.

Let us assume the 13-announcement schedule shown in Table 6.1 that delivers 200 household GRPs is broadcast to all TV homes in the United States. Let us further assume, for simplicity's sake, that there are 95 million homes with TV sets in the United States. Using the first method for calculating impressions, we would multiply the 200 GRPs

Table 7.1 Calculating Impressions

	Households (in 1,000s)	Announcements in Schedule	Impressions (in 1,000s)
Program A	19,000	2	38,000
Program B	14,250	4	57,000
Program C	23,750	2	47,500
Program D	9,500	5	47,500
Total		13	190,000

*Assumed population base: 95 million homes.

(200 percent) by 95 million homes, yielding a product of 190 million homes, or impressions.

Likewise, the households reached by each program, multiplied by the number of announcements in that program, will yield 190 million impressions.

Impressions, like GRPs and TRPs, indicate the *gross* delivery without regard to multiple exposure to the same households or persons. The 13-announcement schedule will be seen by the *equivalent* of 190 million homes, but obviously not by 190 million *different* homes.

As will be discussed later, GRPs and impressions are useful tools for analyzing and buying media, but neither indicates how many *different* people will be exposed to the media forms nor how many *times* they will be exposed. Enter two more terms: reach and frequency.

8

Reach

Reach is the number of *different* individuals (or homes) exposed to a media schedule within a given period of time, generally expressed as a percentage.

Exhibit 8.1 shows a population of 100 TV homes—each box equivalent to one home. Let us assume that you have purchased a schedule of one commercial in each of four different TV programs (A, B, C, and D) that aired in a particular week. Many viewers probably saw more than one announcement. Some of the viewers of Program A might also have viewed Programs B, C, or D or any combination of these. As

Exhibit 8.1. Calculating TV Reach

100 TV Homes

A	A	A	A	A	B	B	B	C	C
C	C	D	D	D	D	D	AB	AB	AC
AC	AD	AD	BC	BC	BD	BD	BD	ABC	ABC
BCD	BCD	BCD	ACD	ACD	ABDC	ABDC	ABDC	ABDC	ABDC

demonstrated, a total of 40 different homes viewed at least one of the programs. The reach of the four programs combined is therefore 40 percent (40 homes reached ÷ 100 TV home population).

To tie back to ratings, we can see that each of the four TV programs have a 20 rating by simply counting the number of homes in which each program was viewed. Program A, for example, was viewed in 20 different homes: 20 homes divided by the 100 TV homes population yields a 20 rating. This schedule of four TV programs, each with a 20 rating, produced 80 GRPs.

To calculate reach, viewers are counted only once, no matter how many programs they view. Also, as a program or programs attract *new* viewers, these viewers contribute to reach.

Exhibit 8.2 displays two TV schedules: one that schedules five spots on the same program (e.g., a talk show that airs daily) and one that schedules five spots on five different programs. With each addi-

Exhibit 8.2. Reach Accumulation of Alternative Schedules

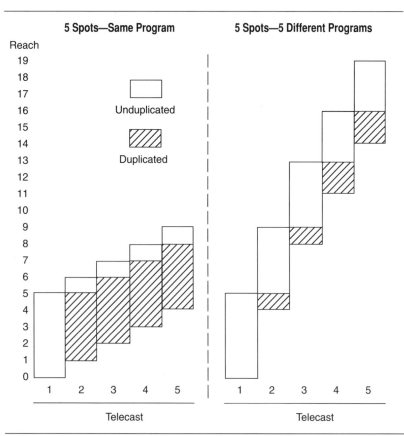

tional spot, new viewers are added—proportionately fewer for the one program schedule and more for the multiprogram schedule. The reason the one program accumulates fewer new viewers has to do with the rate of duplication: there are generally more duplicated viewers of the same program than there are for a combination of different programs.

The dynamics of reach apply to all media forms. The only variation among media is the time frame for which reach is usually expressed. With broadcast media, reach is generally expressed over a four-week period. This is because the data collected by syndicated research sources is usually tabulated over a four-week period for reach calculations. With magazines or newspapers, reach is usually calculated for the total reading audience over the life of a given issue. A weekly magazine, for example, has an average issue life of approximately 4 to 5 weeks. That is, from the time of issuance, it will take about 4 to 5 weeks until the last person who is going to read the magazine reads it. With out-of-home media (outdoor, transit), reach is expressed over a one-month period.

Exhibit 8.3 displays how many women will be reached with an advertising schedule encompassing three magazines. Again, the dynamics of reach are the same as in television but are displayed differently in this exhibit for greater clarification.

Exhibit 8.3. Calculating Magazine Reach

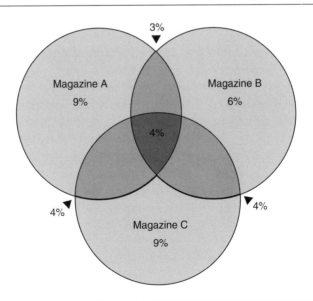

3%

Magazine A
9%

Magazine B
6%

4%

4%

4%

Magazine C
9%

Magazine A is read by 20 percent of all women. Some of these women also read Magazine B or Magazine C, and some read both B and C, as follows:

9%	read *only* A (exclusive audience)
3%	read A and B
4%	read A and C
4%	read A, B, and C
20%	read A

To determine the reach of all three magazines combined, we add the *exclusive* audiences for each to the duplicated audiences, counting the duplicated audience only once:

	Reach
A (exclusive)	9 %
B (exclusive	6
C (exclusive)	9
A + B (duplicated)	3
A + C (duplicated)	4
B + C (duplicated)	4
A + B + C (duplicated)	4
Total	39 %

Reach generally refers to the percentage of people who will be exposed to the advertising media in which commercials or advertisements have been placed. It does not necessarily refer to the percentage of people who will exposed to the actual commercials or ads. When people record their media consumption (via various syndicated research companies' surveys) they record only that they consumed the *vehicle* (the TV program, the radio station, the magazine, etc.), but not that they actually saw/heard a *commercial* or ad. Reaching people with advertising media is therefore an opportunity to expose consumers to advertising. In Europe, for example, reach is referred to as OTS: opportunity to see.

9

Frequency

Frequency is the *average* number of times individuals (or homes) are exposed to advertising messages.

Again, let us use the schedule as originally presented in Exhibit 8.1 in which one commercial was placed in each of four television programs (A, B, C, D). Exhibit 9.1 repeats the pattern of viewing. A total of 40 homes viewed one or more of these four TV programs: 17 homes viewed only 1 program; 11 homes, 2 programs; 7 homes, 3 programs; and 5 homes, 4 programs.

If we add the number of programs each home viewed, the 40 homes in total viewed the *equivalent* of 80 programs and therefore were exposed to the *equivalent* of 80 commercials. By division (80 commercials divided by 40 homes), we establish that the average home was exposed to an average of two commercials.

Average is emphasized for two reasons: First, frequency is often referred to as *average frequency*. Second, *frequency distribution,* an additional concept presented later, is the phenomenon of different groups of people being exposed to media forms with different levels of frequency that are produced by the same advertising schedule.

Exhibit 9.1. Frequency of Advertising Exposure

A	A	A	A	A	B	B	B	C	C
C	C	D	D	D	D	D	AB	AB	AC
AC	AD	AD	BC	BC	BD	BD	BD	ABC	ABC
BCD	BCD	BCD	ACD	ACD	ABDC	ABDC	ABDC	ABDC	ABDC

In Chapter 10 we will reinforce the dynamics described in Exhibit 9.1, namely that the schedule shown produces 80 GRPs, a reach of 40 and an average frequency of 2.0.

Frequency in Print Media

The idea of frequency, like reach, is identical in all media forms. As shown in Exhibit 9.2, Magazines A, B, and C each have exclusive audiences and duplicated audiences. For example, Magazine A is read by 20 percent of the population with 3 percent of this 20 percent also reading Magazine B, 4 percent also reading Magazine C, and 4 percent also reading both Magazines B and C. Magazines B and C have a total readership of 17 percent and 21 percent, respectively. Like Magazine A, both have exclusive and duplicated audiences. In total, the three magazines combined have a *gross* audience of 58 percent (20 + 17 + 21).

If the percent of population that reads one, two, or all three magazines is displayed as in Table 9.1, we can see readily how many people will be exposed to the advertisements one, two, or three times. The number of times they are exposed is the same as the frequency they will receive. In total, 39 percent of the population will be exposed *one or more* times. The average person will be exposed 1.5 times (1.5

Exhibit 9.2. Magazine Frequency

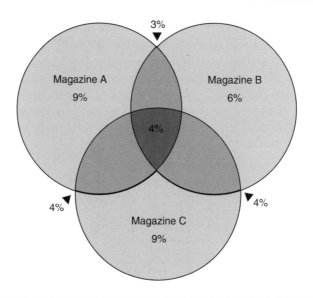

Table 9.1 Percent of People Reached

Magazine	1 Time	2 Times	3 Times
A	9	—	—
B	6	—	—
C	9	—	—
A + B	—	3	—
A + C	—	4	—
B + C	—	4	—
A + B + C	—	—	4
Total	24	11	4
Total—one or more times		39	
Average number of times (Average Frequency)		1.5	

average frequency). This average is obtained by dividing the gross audience (58 percent) by the audience who will be exposed one or more times (39 percent).

Keep in mind that this example of magazine combinations produces 58 GRPs, a 39 reach, and an average frequency of 1.5.

10

Reach/Frequency/GRPs

The three terms work together. Although they are always expressed as a percentage (without the percent sign), they represent the number of people, or homes, that a media schedule will deliver:

- **Reach** tells us *how many* of the audience that you wish to deliver your advertising message(s) to will have the opportunity to be exposed to that advertising (by virtue of the fact that they are consuming the medium in which your advertising appears).

- **Frequency** demonstrates the *average number of times* that audience will be reached (by the media).

- **GRPs** (or **TRPs**) are the product of reach × frequency and will express the *gross* duplicated percentage of audience that will be reached one or more times (by the media).

- **Impressions** indicate the *equivalent number of people* who will be reached one or more times.

Table 10.1 shows a media schedule that delivers an 80 reach with a 2.0 frequency (commonly written as 80/2.0). Total GRPs are therefore 160 (80 × 2.0). Let us assume that the population base against which the R/F was calculated is 10 million. By multiplication we see that the 80 reach equals 8 million people. These 8 million will be exposed to the advertising schedule an average of two times each. Total impression delivery is therefore 16 million (8 million × 2.0).

Table 10.1. Media Schedule

	Percent	Actual
Reach	80.0	80,000,000
Frequency	2.0	—
GRPs	160.0	—
Impressions	—	16,000,000
Total Population	100	10,000,000

How GRPs/TRPs Are Used

GRPs and TRPs are used in two basic ways:

1. To cost-out media schedules, and
2. To calculate reach/frequency.

For print media, a media planner usually calculates the *cost per unit,* such as the cost for a full-page ad. For broadcast media, costs are usually calculated on the basis of *cost per rating point.* The cost-per-point (CPP) is a function of the unit cost divided by the rating of a TV or radio program or time segment: e.g., a $100,000 30-second commercial divided by a rating of 10 yields a CPP of $10,000. (CPP will be discussed in a later chapter.) Knowing the CPP of various segments of television and radio media, the planner can use simple division to determine how many GRPs/TRPs are affordable within a defined media budget. For example, if the budget is $1,000,000 and the estimated CPP is $10,000, the planner is able to schedule 100 GRPs.

Gross rating points are also used to estimate broadcast reach and frequency from tabulations and formulas.

Many researchers have made tabulations that show the reach achieved with different media schedules. These tabulations are put into formulas from which we can estimate the level of delivery (reach) for any given schedule.

Exhibit 10.1 shows the reach curves for typical schedules in two television segments: primetime and daytime. A *reach curve* is the technical term describing the graphic display of reach accumulation with increasing use of a medium.

If we schedule 200 TRPs in primetime television, we would reach approximately 76 percent of women 18–49 years old. Scheduled in daytime television, 200 TRPs would reach about 40 percent of women 18–49. After reach is determined, we can obtain average frequency by dividing the GRPs by the reach:

$$\frac{200 \text{ GRPs}}{40 \text{ Reach}} = 5.0$$

Exhibit 10.1. Accumulation of TV Reach: Women 18–49

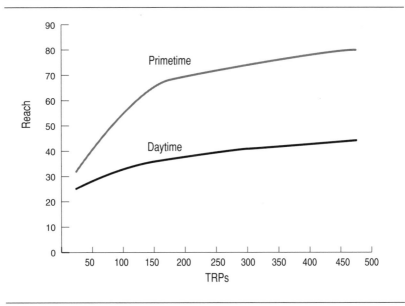

Exhibit 10.1 shows that the line of accumulation *curves* as more and more TRPs are scheduled. The reason for this is that the rate of duplication increases as more TRPs are scheduled. There is an increasingly greater chance that the programs added to a TV schedule (or additional spots in the same programs) will reach duplicated audiences, i.e., those already reached by the previously scheduled programs. As TRPs increase, there are diminishing returns on reach.

Reach/Frequency in TV

Reach and frequency are dependent to a large degree on scheduling patterns. For example, concentration of commercials in a few programs will deliver more frequency and less reach. Conversely, a schedule encompassing a lengthy list of programs will tend to increase reach but deliver less frequency.

Table 10.2 shows that a schedule of 100 TRPs airing within a four-week period in daytime TV will reach 40 percent of women an average of 2.5 times each. The table demonstrates *averages* based on a specific formula. Different formulas can produce different results, albeit all formulas produce approximately the same answers. Some formulas work with generalities while others are sensitive to specific scheduling patterns.

Table 10.2. Reach/Frequency at Different TRP Levels (TV)

	100 TRPs	200 TRPs	300 TRPs	400 TRPs
		Women 18 & Older		
Daytime	40/2.5	45/4.4	48/6.3	50/8.0
Primetime	50/2.0	65/3.1	75/4.0	80/5.0
Late Night	30/3.3	35/5.7	38/7.9	40/10.0
		Men 18 & Older		
Daytime	NT	NT	NT	NT
Primetime	49/2.0	64/3.1	74/4.1	79/5.1
Late Night	29/3.4	34/5.8	37/8.1	39/10.2

NT: Not tabulated.

A generality, for example, might be scheduling 20 commercials in 9 to 12 different programs with each program receiving 1 to 3 spots. A specific scheduling pattern might call for scheduling these same 20 spots in 15 to 20 different programs (known as *high dispersion*), or in 4 to 8 different programs (*low dispersion*). A high dispersion schedule will produce relatively higher reach (and less frequency), while a low dispersion schedule will produce less reach and more frequency.

Reach/frequency in the table is displayed separately for women and men. As discussed earlier, a rating can be calculated for individual demographic groups; therefore, TRPs can be tallied for individual groups. Because viewing habits vary among demographic groups, the reach accumulation pattern for each group also often varies. Additionally, you'll note that the reach levels (for women and men) are highest in primetime (when PUT levels are the highest) and lowest in late night (when PUT levels are lower).

Reach/Frequency in Cable TV

The same dynamics drive cable TV reach/frequency and television overall, i.e., TRP levels and scheduling patterns. However, two phenomena affect the rate and magnitude of cable TV's reach/frequency accumulation: *share*/fragmentation and *penetration*.

Despite the fact that people in homes with cable TV have more program choices, they continue to spend the majority of TV viewing time on broadcast programming. Cable programming has a lower overall share of viewing, which has the effect of depressing reach accumulation. Further, there are more programming choices with cable TV, i.e., the viewer can choose between broadcast programming and a multitude of cable programs. This leads to *fragmentation;* audiences are split into relatively small parcels of population for each program, i.e., the rating for each program is comparatively low and the total reach any one program can yield is likewise comparatively low. Although cable programming offers greater audience targetability, the total reach of any specific program is generally less than can be obtained with the average broadcast program. With the same number of TRPs placed in broadcast TV and cable TV, broadcast generally produces a higher level of reach than cable.

As will be discussed in the chapter "Major Media Forms," only two-thirds of TV households have cable TV (compared to 100 percent of TV households who are able to receive broadcast television). Because the penetration level of cable TV is less than 100 percent (see Table 10.3), reach/frequency for cable TV can be displayed in two ways: (1) against the cable universe, or (2) against the total TV universe. When shown against the total TV universe, the reach is adjusted downward to reflect the fact that there is zero reach against one-third of the universe. As shown in Table 10.5, a schedule of 25 weekly men 25–49

Table 10.3 Share of 24-Hour Viewing by Type of Programming

	Cable Origination	Broadcast Origination
All Cable Households	41%	59%
Noncable Households	—	100%
Average TV Household	29%	71%

Source: Cabletelevision Advertising Bureau; author's estimates.

Table 10.4 Average Ratings of Broadcast and Cable Programming

Programming	Women 18–49, Average Rating
Broadcast TV:	
Early morning	2.1
Daytime	3.5
Primetime	6.9
Late night	2.7
Cable TV (Average women-oriented program)	.7

Source: A. C. Nielsen; Cabletelevision Advertising Bureau.

Table 10.5. Reach/Frequency of Cable TV among Men 25–49

Universe = Cable Households		Universe = All TV Households	
Weekly TRPs	Weekly R/F	Weekly TRPs	Weekly R/F
25	19/1.3	16	12/1.3
50	29/1.7	33	19/1.7
75	36/2.1	49	23/2.1
100	40/2.5	65	26/2.5

Source: Telmar; author's estimates.

TRPs purchased against a cable universe is equivalent, in the *average market,* to 16 TRPs against a total TV universe. "Average market" is emphasized to reinforce the fact that R/F patterns can vary from one market to another based on the percentage of homes in the market that have cable TV. Basically, the higher the cable penetration, the higher the relative reach among a universe of all TV households.

Reach/Frequency in Radio

The dynamics affecting TV R/F patterns also affect radio R/F patterns. Table 10.6 demonstrates reach/frequency at varying levels of TRPs, but this time we display the effect of *dispersion.* At each TRP level the low dispersion schedule (five stations) produces lower reach and higher frequency than the high dispersion schedule (ten stations).

Here again we are still working with averages. The average in this example is that each station has an assumed 1.0 rating for a particular audience segment. Just as with TV programs, different radio stations have different ratings, and each station achieves a different rating level by time of day. We saw in the chapter on HUT that radio listening levels are higher during the day and lower at night. We would normally find that different schedules encompassing a different number of radio stations would produce different average rating levels. This would lead to a different number of spots needing to be purchased on each station in order to produce a set number of TRPs. This, in turn, could affect the reach accumulation pattern. Additionally, Table 10.6 reports the findings in a particular market (Chicago) that has 28 radio stations listed in the audience research reports provided by Arbitron. A market with fewer or more stations could produce substantially different reach/frequency patterns.

Reach/frequency for radio, as for most media, is tabulated for the specific geographic area in which the medium delivers an audience.

Table 10.6. Reach/Frequency in Radio Based on Dispersion Level

	100 TRPs		200 TRPs		300 TRPs		400 TRPs	
# of Stations:	5	10	5	10	5	10	5	10
TRPs/Station	20	10	40	20	60	30	80	40
Reach	35	40	40	55	43	63	45	67
Frequency	2.9	2.5	5.0	3.6	7.0	4.8	8.9	5.9

Source: KATZ Radio.

For radio the listening audience is considered to be within the Metro area. Radio's true reach potential usually extends beyond the geographic boundaries of the Metro area, but lack of research information and various other methodological problems prevent R/F analysis for the total area covered by radio stations. If a planned schedule is estimated to reach 50 percent of a target audience in a market of 100,000 people, chances are that the absolute audience delivery will exceed 50,000, i.e., there will be people outside of the Metro area who will also be reached. In Chapter 23 ("Geographic Areas") the topic of radio's *Total Survey Area* will continue.

Reach/Frequency in Out-of-Home Media

The starting point for estimating reach/frequency of out-of-home media is also GRPs. The typical outdoor purchase is made on the basis of daily GRPs, and reach/frequency is calculated for a month-long period.

The R/F of outdoor advertising is affected by many factors, such as:

- The physical dimensions of the advertisement. For example, a *painted bulletin* measuring 12 feet by 48 feet usually is more visible and can attract more people than a *one-sheet poster* measuring 2 feet by 4 feet.

- The location. For example, a painted bulletin located next to a major highway tends to be exposed to more people than a one-sheet on the side of a building wall.

- The level of GRPs purchased. As with all media, the greater the quantity (e.g., GRPs) the greater the reach or frequency or both.

- The general availability of people who could be exposed to the medium. For example, people age 18–49 commute to and from

Table 10.7. Reach/Frequency of Outdoor Advertising

		One Month Reach/Frequency	
Type of Buy	Daily GRPs	Men 18+	Women 18+
30 Sheet Posters	50	89/17.7	86/14.5
	100	94/33.4	93/26.9
Permanent Paints	50	72/21.7	67/18.5
	100	84/37.4	81/30.9

Source: Patrick Media: Gallup model.

work in greater numbers than people 65 and older and there-fore are more likely to be exposed to an out-of-home adver-tisement.

Table 10.7 demonstrates average reach/frequency for men and women at two GRP levels for two types of outdoor buys. A discussion of these and other types of outdoor buys is presented later.

Reach/Frequency in Print Media

Because of the nature of the audience data collected by syndicated research companies, GRPs do not have to be used to estimate reach and frequency for print media.

Syndicated research companies, such as Simmons and MRI, collect readership information for a long list of publications. The data is also reported on the basis of duplicated readership—how many people read both Magazine A and Magazine B, both Magazine A and Magazine C, etc., as was demonstrated in Exhibit 9.2. These *duplication rates* are used in various mathematical formulas to determine the reach of combinations of magazines. The formulas are complex and usually require a computer program to accomplish the calculations. Most magazines have access to the computer programs, as do most media planners, either through their own proprietary systems or through research service companies such as Telmar or Interactive Market Systems.

Magazines and newspapers accumulate new audiences with successive issues just as a TV program accumulates new viewers with successive episodes. And just as TV ratings reflect the average audience during the duration of a TV program, so a publication's audience count is based on the average issue. The average audience for a magazine or newspaper is composed of frequent (loyal) readers, who read nearly every issue, as well as infrequent readers, who happened to read the issue(s) studied by the media researcher. With successive issues of a publication we find audience *turnover:* new subscribers replacing those who stopped subscribing, new infrequent readers, etc.

Table 10.8 indicates the audience *build* for successive issues of an average magazine, and what portion of the cumulative reach is accounted for by "new" readers and by "duplicated" readers. The table is based on a 10 rating, i.e., this magazine reaches 10 percent of a certain demographic group with its average issue. As shown, two issues of the same magazine accumulate a total reach of 13.8 (percent). Of the average issue reach of 10 added by the second insertion, 6.2 of the reach points are accounted for by the same people who were reached by the first issue (62 percent duplication) and 3.8 of the reach points are accounted for by new readers (those not reached by the first issue).

Similar dynamics affect newspaper reach/frequency patterns, although there are technicalities unique to the medium that could produce different overall reach/frequency results. Of the following four points, the first three apply to an individual newspaper. The fourth point applies to combinations of newspapers.

1. There is proportionately more audience turnover for the average daily newspaper versus the average magazine because news-

Table 10.8. Audience Accumulation and Source of Audience for Successive Issues of a Magazine

| | | | Source of Additional Audience | | | |
| | | | Duplicated Readers | | New Readers | |
# of Issues	TRPs per Issue	Cumulative Reach	Reach	%	Reach	%
1	10.0	10.0	—	—	10.0	100
2	10.0	13.8	6.2	62	3.8	38
3	10.0	16.0	7.8	78	2.2	22
4	10.0	17.5	8.5	85	1.5	15
5	10.0	18.5	9.0	90	1.0	10
Total	50.0	18.5			18.5	

Source: MRI; Telmar; author's estimates.

papers have proportionately more readers who purchase a single copy (via newsstands) rather than subscribe. With single-copy sales there's more audience *churn*: With successive issues, there are new readers buying today's issue and yesterday's readers not buying today's issue. Therefore, the audience *build* is relatively greater.

2. The larger daily newspapers in each market tend to have a larger reach (coverage) than the average magazine. The larger the reach of an average issue, the less opportunity to attract new readers; therefore, the audience build is proportionately lower. For example, a publication that reaches 5 percent of adults has an opportunity to build reach from the remaining 95 percent; a publication with a higher average issue reach has less remaining opportunity.

3. The average newspaper issue has less *passalong* than the average magazine issue. This is due for the most part to the short-lived editorial of newspapers. Yesterday's news does not have to be read when there is new news today. This limits the eventual reach potential of the average daily.

4. Newspapers have proportionately less audience duplication than magazines. Most newspaper readers read only one daily newspaper. Therefore, additional newspapers scheduled in a market tend to contribute proportionately more to reach accumulation than to average frequency.

Table 10.9 displays newspaper reach/frequency by issue for a schedule encompassing up to five issues of a multipaper buy in the top ten markets. In this buy a total of 85 TRPs are generated with each issue.

Table 10.9. Reach Accumulation for Multinewspaper, Multi-Issue Schedule

# of Issues	Each Day			Cumulative		
	TRPs	Reach	Frequency	TRPs	Reach	Frequency
1	85	67	1.3	85	67	1.3
2	85	67	1.3	170	77	2.2
3	85	67	1.3	255	85	3.0
4	85	67	1.3	340	89	3.8
5	85	67	1.3	425	91	4.7

Source: Newspaper Association of America.

Total reach for the first issue is 67 (indicating a 21 duplication rate for all papers combined: 85 − 67 = 18 ÷ 85 = 21%). Like magazines, reach accumulates as successive issues are added. Note that the rate of reach accumulation is less for this schedule of newspapers than for the previous schedule for magazines.

How Reach and Frequency Are Used

Reach and frequency are used in several ways:

- As a simple reporting device. For example, a specific plan might reveal that during the average month 75 percent of the target audience will be reached an average of four times, i.e., a 75/4.0 reach/frequency, thereby giving the advertiser a sense of how much media delivery will be generated.

- To establish a goal against which media plan alternatives are constructed. For example, a planner might set out to achieve a certain level of reach or frequency, or reach/frequency, and devise media tactics that can produce the desired level.

- To compare alternatives within a medium, or media mix alternatives. For example, R/F can be used to judge the effect of different daypart combinations in TV or radio, or different combinations of print media, or different combinations of different media forms.

The following example addresses the third point: using R/F to compare intramedia alternatives; it can equally apply to any planning options. Table 10.10 shows two alternative schedules, both of which

Table 10.10. Reach/Frequency Comparisons

	Plan I		Plan II	
	# of: 30 Spots	Women 18–49 TRPs	# of: 30 Spots	Women 18–49 TRPs
Primetime	10	70	5	50
Daytime	20	70	37	130
Total	30	140	42	180
Reach		50		45
Frequency		2.8		4.0

cost the same amount of money. Plan I schedules ten 30-second announcements (also called *spots*) in primetime (generally 8–11 P.M. EST) network TV and 20 spots in daytime network TV. Plan II has five spots in prime and 37 in daytime. Plan II delivers more spots, more women 18–49 TRPs, and more frequency. Plan I, however, has the edge on reach. In deciding between these alternatives, the media planner must choose which is more important: reach or frequency. The number of spots produced by either plan has nothing to do with the decision about R/F. The number of spots is merely a device for calculating TRPs (i.e., an average primetime rating of 7.0 × 10 spots equals 70 TRPs; an average daytime rating of 3.5 × 20 spots also equals 70 TRPs).

Discussed in the next chapter, entitled "Media Mix," are the concepts of *only only both* and the dynamics of adding together two different media forms.

How Impressions Are Used

Like gross rating points, impressions also indicate *total* delivery without regard to duplication. Impressions are used to demonstrate delivery of alternative schedules.

Table 10.11 shows two plans at equal budgets. Both plans deliver 120 million home impressions. If we were interested only in homes, with both plans producing the same impressions, we would be hard pressed to select the better plan. If we were concerned with women, Plan I would be superior, because it delivers more women impressions. If women 18 to 34 years old were of primary consideration, Plan II would have the advantage.

Another use for impression data is to compare the *audience composition* of a media plan's delivery to its objectives to determine if

Table 10.11. Comparison of Alternative Plans with Equal Expenditures

	Impressions (in 1,000s)	
	Plan I	Plan II
Total homes	120,000	120,000
Total women	90,000	85,000
18–34	30,000	40,000
35–49	30,000	30,000
50 & older	30,000	15,000

Table 10.12. Impression Comparison of Two Plans

	% Total Impressions		
	Objective	**Plan I**	**Plan II**
Total women	100 %	100 %	100 %
18–34	50	33	47
35–49	25	33	35
50 & older	25	33	17

delivery is in the relative proportion desired. (Audience composition is also discussed later.)

As shown in Table 10.12, Plan I delivers impressions in a flat pattern—equal delivery to each age grouping. Plan II, with 47 percent of impressions accounted for by women 18 to 34, is biased to delivery to younger women and therefore more closely approximates the objectives of the media plan.

A dilemma could arise if, when comparing alternative media plans, the planner finds that one plan delivers more impressions to the primary audience being sought, while the other media plan delivers fewer impressions to this group but a greater percentage of the *total* impressions.

The answer is complicated and, at the same time, easy. The reader should have a sense at this point in the book that many variables are involved in analyzing media forms and devising a media plan. No one variable (reach, frequency, impressions, etc.) should ever be the only criterion for decision making. Additionally, as we shall see, a number of methods exist for dealing with each of the variables in combination whereby a *valued* decision can be made.

11

Media Mix

Media mix refers to the use of two or more different media forms in one advertising plan.

There are a number of reasons for mixing media. Among the most common are:

- To reach people not reached with the first medium.

- To provide additional repeat exposure in a less expensive, secondary medium after optimum reach is obtained in the first medium.

- To utilize some of the intrinsic values of a medium to extend the creative effectiveness of the advertising campaign (such as music on radio or long copy in print media).

- To deliver coupons in print media when the primary media vehicle in the media plan is broadcast.

- *Synergism*, a term borrowed from chemistry, which describes an effect produced by the sum of the parts that is greater than that expected by adding together the individual components.

When two media forms are combined to increase total reach, the basic supposition is that the secondary medium provides advertising exposure opportunities beyond those offered by the first medium—the first medium, based on its usage in your media plan, has limited reach.

In Exhibit 11.1, 60 percent of the population is reached with a specific television schedule. This means 40 percent is not reached by that TV schedule. Additionally, a specific magazine schedule reaches

Exhibit 11.1. Media Mix Reach

Television	60% Reached	40% Not Reached

Magazines	30% Not Reached	50% Reached	20% Not Reached

Either/Or	80% Reached	20% Not Reached

50 percent of people, meaning 50 percent are not reached with these magazines (30 percent + 20 percent, shown in separate bars for demonstration purposes).

An accepted statistical method for combining the reach of these two media is *random combination,* which assumes that those not reached by one medium have an opportunity to be exposed to the second medium. This opportunity increases as the proportion of those not reached by the first medium increases. Using the random technique, we can establish that 20 percent of people are not reached by either medium:

40%	not reached in television
× 50%	not reached in magazines
20%	not reached by either medium

Subtracting 20 percent from the total possible reach of 100 percent leaves 80 percent, which is the percentage the combination in this schedule supposedly *does* reach.

One last point. When combining two or more media forms, you must establish reach for all media on the same population base. You cannot combine the reach of women in one medium with that of men in another medium. Nor can you combine the reach of homes equipped with cable television in a television schedule with that of total homes for a newspaper plan. In this instance, you must either calculate reach for the television plan for total homes, or calculate reach of the newspaper plan for homes equipped with cable television.

Exhibit 11.2 shows the combined reach of two media forms using the random combination technique. Referring to the previous example of a television and magazine plan, we can use this table to estimate total reach of the two media combined:

- Find the reach of the first medium on the horizontal axis—60.

Exhibit 11.2. Combined Reach of Two Media

Reach of One Medium

		25	30	35	40	45	50	55	60	65	70	75	80	85	90	95
	25	46	47	51	55	59	62	66	70	74	77	81	85	89	92	95
	30	—	51	54	58	61	65	68	72	75	79	82	86	90	93	95
	35	—	—	58	61	64	67	71	74	77	80	84	87	90	93	95
	40	—	—	—	64	67	70	73	76	79	82	85	88	91	94	95
	45	—	—	—	—	70	72	75	78	81	83	86	89	92	94	95
Reach of Second Medium	50	—	—	—	—	—	75	77	80	82	85	87	90	92	95	95
	55	—	—	—	—	—	—	80	82	84	86	89	91	93	95	95
	60	—	—	—	—	—	—	—	84	86	88	90	92	94	95	95
	65	—	—	—	—	—	—	—	—	88	89	91	93	95	95	95
	70	—	—	—	—	—	—	—	—	—	91	92	94	95	95	95
	75	—	—	—	—	—	—	—	—	—	—	94	95	95	95	95
	80	—	—	—	—	—	—	—	—	—	—	—	95	95	95	95
	85	—	—	—	—	—	—	—	—	—	—	—	—	95	95	95
	90	—	—	—	—	—	—	—	—	—	—	—	—	—	95	95
	95	—	—	—	—	—	—	—	—	—	—	—	—	—	—	95

- Find the reach of the second medium on the vertical axis—50.

- Read down from the 60 reach on the horizontal axis, and across from the 50 reach on the vertical axis. The point of intersection shows the combined reach—80.

If three media forms are combined, the same procedure is used: find the combined reach of the first two media, then find the reach of this combination plus the third medium:

	REACH
Medium A	60
Medium B	50
Medium A & B	80 (from Table 11.2)
Medium C	35
Medium A & B & C	87 (from Table 11.2)

Only Only Both

We can also analyze media combinations in terms of the percentage that will receive only the first medium, or only the second medium, or both media.

This calculation should always be made to show exposure to each media form being used. It is often mistakenly assumed that when two media are combined, all people reached will be exposed to your advertising in *both* media. The usual effect of adding a second medium is to extend reach to those not exposed to the first medium.

To calculate "only-only-both" reach, use the following procedure:

1. Combine the two media randomly:

$$60\% + 50\% = 80\%$$

2. Subtract the reach of medium A (60%) from the combined reach (80%)— this yields the percentage exposed to only medium B (20%):

$$80\% - 60\% = 20\%$$

3. Subtract the reach of medium B (50%) from the combined reach (80%)— this yields the percentage exposed to only medium A (30%):

$$80\% - 50\% = 30\%$$

4. Subtract the combined reach of only medium A (30%) and only medium B (20%) from the total combined reach (80%)—this yields the percentage exposed to *both* media (30%):

$$80\% - (20\% + 30\%) = 30\%$$

If the media forms in the media plan are those shown in Exhibit 11.3, the planner can conclude the following:

- Television will reach 60 percent of the population against which these calculations have been made.

- Magazines will reach 50 percent.

- 80 percent will be reached by TV, or magazines, or both.

- 30 percent will be reached by TV *only*.

Exhibit 11.3. Media Mix Reach

Television	60% Reached		40% Not Reached	

Magazines	30% Not Reached	50% Reached	20% Not Reached	

Either/Or	80% Reached		20% Not Reached	

	TV Only 30%	TV & Mags 30%	Mags Only 20%	20% Not Reached

- 20 percent will be reached by magazines *only.*

- 30 percent will be reached by *both* TV and magazines.

- 20 percent of the population will not be reached with this advertising schedule.

After you have established the combined reach of all media, calculating the average frequency is a simple matter. Simply add the TRPs of all media combined and divide by the combined reach. For example:

	Reach	Frequency		TRPs	
TV	60	×	5.0	=	300
Magazines	50	×	3.0	=	150
Total	80				450

450 ÷ 80 Reach = 5.6 Frequency

12

Frequency Distribution

Frequency distribution is the array of reach at each frequency level. Perhaps a more descriptive name for this concept is *reach at each frequency level.*

We have noted that during an advertising campaign people are reached with different rates of exposure. For example, when we spoke of magazine reach and frequency, we saw that some people read only one magazine, some read two, and some read three. This resulted in a frequency level of 1.0, 2.0, and 3.0, respectively. Further, the reach for each of these frequency levels was also shown—indicating that 24 percent of the people were exposed to the media *only* once, 11 per-

Table 12.1. Frequency Distribution

Schedule:	Primetime TV—10 spots (70 Women 18–49 TRPs)	
	Daytime TV—20 spots (70 Women 18–49 TRPs)	
	Frequency	**Reach**
	1	15
	2	12
	3	9
	4	6
	5	3
	6	2
	7	1
	8	1
	9	1
	Total Reach	50
	Average Frequency	2.8
	TRPs	140

cent *only* twice, and 4 percent *only* three times. That example illustrates the concept of frequency distribution.

In the advertising campaign illustrated in Table 12.1, 30 spots are used in a combination of primetime and daytime TV. In total, 50 percent of Women 18–49 would be reached with this schedule (one or more times). The "more" has to do with average frequency and with frequency distribution. The *average* woman reached would be exposed to 2.8 commercials. Some will receive less than this level of exposure; some will receive a higher level of exposure.

As shown, 15 percent of this target audience will be exposed to *only* one airing of the commercial, 12 percent will be exposed to *only* two commercials, and so forth. By adding the reach at each frequency level we arrive at the total reach of 50.

13

Effective Reach

Effective reach is the number of individuals (or homes) reached by a media schedule *at a given level of frequency.* Effective reach is also commonly called *effective frequency.*

Although no definitive and universally accepted research quantifies the value of each exposure level (i.e., how much greater is the advertising value of a consumer seeing four advertising messages versus two messages), judgment suggests that the values are different. Furthermore, because of the absolute costs of purchasing media, care should be taken not to spend more, or less, than is necessary to deliver advertising effectively.

Some research has been conducted on the relationship between frequency of exposure and advertising effectiveness. An Association of National Advertisers publication summarizes most of the industry research conducted in this area.[1] The author, Michael J. Naples, draws 12 conclusions from his analysis of the research. The conclusions are listed below to reinforce the concept of effective reach (frequency):

1. One exposure of an advertisement to a target group consumer within a purchase cycle has little or no effect in all but a minority of circumstances.

2. Since one exposure is usually ineffective, the central goal of productive media planning should be to place emphasis on enhancing frequency rather than reach.

---

[1] Michael Naples, *Effective Frequency: The Relationship Between Frequency and Advertising Effectiveness.* Association of National Advertisers, New York, NY, 1988.

3. The weight of evidence suggests strongly that an exposure frequency of two within a purchase cycle is an effective level.

4. By and large, optimal exposure frequency appears to be at least three exposures within a purchase cycle.

5. Beyond three exposures within a brand purchase cycle, or during a period of four or even eight weeks . . . increasing frequency continues to build advertising effectiveness at a decreasing rate, but with no evidence of a decline.

6. The frequency-of-exposure data from this review strongly suggests that wearout is not a function of too much frequency   per se.

7. . . . Very large and well-known brands—and/or those with dominant market shares in their categories and dominant shares of category advertising weight—appear to differ markedly in response to frequency of exposure from smaller or more average brands.

8. Perhaps as a result of the differing exposure environments of television dayparts, frequency of exposure . . . has a differential effect on advertising response by daypart.

9. . . . The amount of money a brand spends on advertising as a percent of total category advertising expenditures has a significant positive effect on brand users' purchase probabilities.

10. Nothing we have seen suggests that frequency response principles or generalizations vary by medium.

11. Although there are general principles with respect to frequency of exposure and its relationship to advertising effectiveness, differential effects by brand are equally important.

12. . . . The leverage of different equal-expenditure media plans in terms of frequency response can be substantial.

Naples' fourth conclusion: "at least three exposures within a purchase cycle" is most notable. Certainly, the purchase cycle varies by product category (e.g., milk versus a car), and so the timing between the first and third exposure should also vary.

The three-exposure level was a concept presented by Dr. Herbert Krugman.[2] Krugman theorized that three exposures to a TV commer-

---

[2]Herbert E. Krugman, "Why Three Exposures May Be Enough," *Journal of Advertising Research,* December 1972: 11–14.

cial might be the basic number needed for effective communication. His "Three Hit" theory is now commonly referred to as *Reach at 3+*. Although it is only theory, and although it referred only to television advertising as it was more than two decades ago, Reach at 3+ has taken hold and often permeates many media decisions.

Three hits is used mostly as a matter of convenience among the uninitiated. Three hits cannot possibly apply to every advertising campaign in every medium. Judgment is needed in deciding how many advertising exposures are needed for effective communication. Notwithstanding the dilemma of not knowing how many advertising exposures are needed, the reader should conclude that an analysis of media schedule alternatives based on average frequency is both deficient and possibly misleading.

Two different media plans might produce the same average frequency but perform completely differently in terms of delivering as many consumers as possible at a predetermined level of frequency. Therefore, whenever possible, media schedules should be analyzed according to frequency distribution, and values should be placed on varying exposure levels.

What value should be placed on each frequency level? That's the media planner's judgment. No one knows how many exposures are needed for effective communication, and even if this was known, it probably would not apply to all consumer products and services, and probably not to all media forms. Some of the many questions that must be answered before values are assigned include:

- Is this a well-established, well-known brand, or a new brand entering the market?

- Is the product's competition fierce or tranquil?

- Is the creative message simple or complex?

- Will the advertising be placed in a highly cluttered or relatively uncluttered medium?

After we determine the value of given exposure levels, plans can be evaluated based on effective reach. Two methods could be employed:

1. Determine the reach at the desired frequency level(s).

2. Place a value on various frequency levels.

The Reach at the Desired Frequency Level(s)

As shown in the frequency distribution example (Table 12.1), 50 percent of Women 18 to 49 will be exposed to one or more commercials. To establish how many will be exposed to two or more, three or more, etc., simply add the reach at each frequency level to the reach for the previous frequency level, starting at the highest level of frequency (the bottom of the chart):

	Reach at frequency level of 9	=	1
+	Reach at frequency level of 8	=	1
	Reach at frequency level of 8 or more	=	2

If the planner decides that the minimum effective frequency level is, for example, 4, then this particular schedule would generate a reach of 14 at the 4 or more frequency level. Comparing this schedule to alternative plans could determine which plan produces the highest level of reach at the 4 or more level. Likewise, the planner might also decide that a *range* of frequency levels should be used for this analysis. In this instance the planner would choose the amount of reach generated within this range. For example, if the desired frequency range is 2 to 6, this schedule produces a 32 reach.

Table 13.1. Method #1 To Determine Effective Reach

Schedule: Primetime TV—10 spots (70 Women 18–49 TRPs)
                    Daytime TV—20 spots (70 Women 18–49 TRPs)

Reach at Individual Levels		Reach at Cumulative Levels	
Frequency	Reach	Frequency	Reach
1	15	1 or more	50
2	12	2 or more	35
3	9	3 or more	23
4	6	4 or more	14
5	3	5 or more	8
6	2	6 or more	5
7	1	7 or more	3
8	1	8 or more	2
9	1	9 or more	1

The Value of Various Frequency Levels

Determine the value of each frequency level (or range of frequency). For example, it might be judged that women reached with a 3 to 6 frequency are effectively reached, while lower frequency levels produce half as much effectiveness, and higher frequency (although it might still be effective) is judged to not be needed. If this is the decision scenario, these judgments can be quantified and applied to the reach at each frequency grouping. Here again a frequency distribution is needed.

As shown in Table 13.2, the 1–2 frequency range is given a value of 50 percent, the 3-6 range a value of 100 percent, and the 7+ range a value of 90 percent. By multiplying the reach of each frequency grouping by its respective value, and adding the products, we can determine that this schedule produces a 36.2 reach. An alternative value system is displayed on the right side of Table 13.2 to demonstrate that different values will produce different results.

Table 13.2. Method #2 To Determine Effective Reach

| Schedule: | Primetime TV—10 spots (70 Women 18–49 TRPs) | | | | |
| | Daytime TV—20 spots (70 Women 18–49 TRPs) | | | | |

Frequency Range	Women 18–49 Reach	Alternative 1 Values		Alternative 2 Values	
		Value	Reach	Value	Reach
1–2	27	50	13.5	80	21.6
3–6	20	100	20.0	100	20.0
7+	3	90	2.7	100	3.0
Total	50		36.2		44.6

14

Quintile Distribution

A quintile distribution is similar to a frequency distribution, but rather than displaying reach at each frequency level, it groups the audience reached into five equal parts and averages the frequency for each group.

Quintiles are the subject of this chapter, but the same concept applies to any equal divisions of people or homes (e.g., tertile: one-third; decile: one-tenth). Quintiles are discussed here only because many advertisers continue to use the concept. The concept, however, has lost much favor because planners have moved to an assessment of effective reach.

All media forms attract people at different levels of exposure, ranging from those who are heavy consumers of the medium to those who are lightly exposed or not users of the medium at all. The same phenomenon usually occurs with product consumption—ranging from those consumers who buy and use more of a product than the average person to those who do not use the product at all. It is not uncommon, for examples, to see data that reports that 20 percent of the population account for 80 percent of a product's consumption.

Displayed in Table 14.1 is a quintile analysis for men television viewers. One-fifth of men (20 percent of the total population) view 44.7 hours per week, compared to the average weekly viewing for all men of 20.8 hours. For purposes of demonstration, let us assume that each one-fifth of the population is one man. Therefore, if we add the viewing hours of each of these five men, we arrive at the equivalent of 104.1 hours. Dividing the 44.7 hours of the heaviest viewing quintile by the total of 104.1 hours, we determine that these heavy viewers account for 42 percent of all viewing.

Table 14.1. Television Quintile Analysis (Total Viewing—Men)

Quintile	% U.S. Population	Average Hours of Weekly Viewing	% of Total Viewing
Heaviest	20	44.7	42
Next	20	26.4	26
Next	20	18.4	18
Next	20	11.3	11
Lightest	20	3.3	3
Total	100 %	104.1	100 %
Average	—	20.8	—

Source: Simmons.

Calculating a Quintile Distribution

To calculate a quintile distribution, we must first have a complete frequency distribution. In the quintile example shown in Table 14.2, we have used the same frequency distribution used in the previous chapter.

Using this data, the total reach must be divided into five equal parts. In this example, one-fifth of the total 50 reach is a 10 reach. Just as we had accumulated reach from the bottom up in determining

Table 14.2. Frequency Distribution

Frequency	Reach
1	15
2	12
3	9
4	6
5	3
6	2
7	1
8	1
9	1
Total Reach	50
Average Frequency	2.8
TRPs	140

reach at the "1 or more" level, "2 or more level," etc., we also add from the bottom up to calculate a quintile distribution. The idea is to accumulate 10 reach points for each quintile segment. To do this, the reach at certain frequency levels must be apportioned between two

Table 14.3. Television Quintile Analysis

Frequency Distribution		Quintile Distribution			
Frequency	Reach	Reach	TRPs	Frequency	Segment
1	10	10	10	1.0	Lightest
1	5	10	15	1.5	Next
2	5				
2	7	10	23	2.3	Next
3	3				
3	6	10	34	3.4	Next
4	4				
4	2	10	59	5.9	Heaviest
5	3				
6	2				
7	1				
8	1				
9	1				
Total	50	50	140*	2.8	Average

*Rounded to 140 for purposes of demonstration.

Table 14.4. Apportioning Reach to Different Quintiles

Frequency	Reach Shown on Frequency Distribution	Reached Used for Quintile Segment
9	1	1
8	1	1
7	1	1
6	2	2
5	3	3
4	6	2*

*The four remaining reach points (6 - 2 = 4) are used to calculate reach for the next quintile.

different quintile segments. The arithmetic, starting at the bottom of Table 14.3, is shown in Table 14.4.

After the frequency distribution is divided into five equal reach segments, TRPs need to be calculated. The formula is as previously discussed: reach × frequency = TRPs. In this example, the arithmetic (for what is labeled the "heaviest" segment) is as follows:

Frequency		Reach		TRPs
9	×	1	=	9
8	×	1	=	8
7	×	1	=	7
6	×	2	=	12
5	×	3	=	15
4	×	2	=	8
Total				59

The next step is to calculate *average frequency* for each quintile segment. This is accomplished by dividing TRPs by the reach, e.g., 59 TRPs divided by a 10 reach equals 5.9 average frequency.

The last step is designating each segment: the segment with the least amount of average frequency is designated as the lightest viewing quintile; the segment with the most frequency is the heaviest viewing quintile.

Quintile Distributions of a Media Mix

Whenever a second medium is added to the first, the frequency distribution (and therefore the quintile distribution) *flattens*. Disproportionately more frequency is added to the more lightly exposed groups than to the most heavily exposed group.

There is a mistaken belief that heavy users of one medium are automatically light users of another. This appears logical if one concludes that people, in general, spend about the same amount of time each day with their preferred media forms; therefore, if people view television for most of that time, they will have less time to spend with other media. This logic is quantified in Table 14.5. Here we see a two-way *tertile distribution*—one set of tertiles for TV and another for radio. Each tertile accounts for one-third of the users of the respective medium.

Table 14.5 is read as follows: Of all radio listeners who are considered "heavy" users of the medium, 20 percent are also "heavy" TV

Table 14.5. Mistaken Logic Surrounding Intermedia Audiences

TV Tertiles	% of Each Radio Tertile Contained in Each TV Tertile		
	Heavy	**Moderate**	**Light**
Heavy	20 %	35 %	50 %
Moderate	30	30	30
Light	50	35	20
Total	100 %	100 %	100 %

Table 14.6 Intermedia Audiences

TV Tertiles	% of Each Radio Tertile Contained in Each TV Tertile		
	Heavy	**Moderate**	**Light**
Heavy	33 %	33 %	33 %
Moderate	34	34	34
Light	33	33	33
Total	100 %	100 %	100 %

viewers. Further, most of the "light" radio listeners (50 percent) are "heavy" TV viewers.

While logical, this is not a real-world phenomenon. The fact is that people spend varying amounts of time with media. Some are heavy consumers of media overall; some are light consumers. As a result of this pattern, consumers of one medium (e.g., magazine readers) have an equal propensity to be heavy, moderate, or light consumers of another medium. This real-world situation is displayed in Table 14.6.

Table 14.6 is read as follows: Of all radio listeners who are considered "heavy" users of the medium, one-third (33 percent) are also "heavy" TV viewers. Overall, if a person is a heavy, moderate, or light listener to radio, that person tends to be equally represented in each of the heavy, moderate, and light viewing tertiles.

Because of what happens in the real world, the frequency distribution tends to flatten whenever a second medium is added to the first. Adding magazines to a base of television, for example, delivers equal frequency to each TV quintile but disproportionately more frequency to the lighter viewing quintiles than to the heavier viewing quintiles. As shown in Exhibit 14.1, the addition of magazines increases frequency among the lightest viewing one-fifth by 200 percent,

Exhibit 14.1. Quintile Distribution—Adding a Second Medium

		Percent Increase in Frequency
Lightest	1.0 · 2.0	200%
Next	1.7 · 2.0	118
Next	2.7 · 2.0	74
Next	4.3 · 2.0	47
Heaviest	7.3 · 2.0	27

Television ☐   Magazines ▨

compared with a 27 percent increase in frequency of the heaviest viewing one-fifth.

In this example, television provides a frequency of 1.0 to the lightest quintile, 1.7 to the next quintile, up to a 7.3 average frequency to the heaviest viewing quintile of reach. Magazines, with an average frequency of 2.0, deliver the same level of frequency to each of the TV viewing quintiles.

If additional television were scheduled in lieu of a second medium, the quintile distribution would have the same configuration as shown for television alone. The absolute level of frequency would increase proportionately across each of the quintiles.

The same dynamics operate regardless of which two media forms are used. More of the same medium results in a quintile distribution that delivers significantly more frequency to the heavy consumers of that medium than to the lighter users. A second medium always disproportionately increases the frequency among the lighter users of the first medium.

Quintile distributions are a better designator of frequency among different groups of people than average frequency but less discriminating than a complete frequency distribution. Nevertheless, quintile distributions are used periodically to assess the dynamics of a media schedule, to determine the impact of a second medium, or to decide when an additional commercial should be put into the pool of commercials being aired. Judgment dictates how many exposures are sufficient, or too few, or too many.

15

Index

An index is a form of percentage that relates numbers to a base, with the base being 100. It is used to demonstrate quickly what is average, above average, or below average in terms of the magnitude of difference among numbers.

Let us assume we need to define the age profile of female consumers of Product X. We want to determine which of the age groups have the greatest relative concentrations of users so we can properly select media to reach them. This procedure can be done in a number of ways. An index is one of the ways.

Table 15.1 indicates that there are 120 million females aged 12 and older in the United States, and 18 million (15 percent) of them used Product X. Likewise, of the 12 million females aged 12 to 17, 1.1 million purchased Product X. A review of the number of females who used Product X reveals that those aged 35 to 49 represent the greatest

Table 15.1. Calculating an Index

	Population		Product X Users		
	Number (in millions)	% Total	Number (in millions)	% Total	Index
12–17	12.0	10.0	1.1	6.1	61
18–24	14.4	12.0	2.5	13.9	116
25–34	24.0	20.0	4.5	25.0	125
35–49	33.6	28.0	5.0	27.8	99
50+	36.0	30.0	4.9	27.2	91
Total	120.0	100.0	18.0	100.0	100

number of users (5 million), but overlooks the fact that these females also represent a very large population group (33.6 million people representing 28 percent of the total U.S. female population base). By relating the *percent* of Product X users who are 35 to 49 to the *percent* population of females in the same age group we discover that this age group is *average,* i.e., both usage and population are at the 28 percent level; their usage level of Product X is on par with the U.S. average.

By comparing the two sets of columns (percent total population and percent of total Product X users), we can see that *proportionately* more females aged 18 to 24 and 25 to 34 use Product X than found in the population at large, e.g., the 18 to 24 group equals 13.9 percent of users and 12.0 percent of the population. In going through long statistical tables, one could cite where there is a higher, average, or lower relative concentration by observing each percentage. Using addition and subtraction we can display how many percentage points above or below average any particular age cell is. For example, we can subtract 13.9 percent from 12.0 percent and, arriving at 1.9 percentage difference, determine that this age cell is proportionately greater than average.

The easier method is to calculate an index to determine the proportional relationships. By dividing the 25.0 percent (for female Product X users aged 25 to 34) by 12.0 percent (population), we arrive at a quotient of 1.25. By moving the decimal point two places to the right, we have calculated an *index.* In this case the index states that there is a 25 percent greater concentration of females who used Product X in the 25 to 34 age group than is found in the general population.

Note that the index includes the 100 percent representing the base. Also note that the percent sign is deleted when referring to an index:

Base (12.0% of population)		100 %
% increase	+	25 %
Total		125 %
Index		125

An index of 100 indicates an average concentration (or average relationship). Indices above and below 100 indicate concentrations that are higher or lower than average, respectively. The numerical difference between a higher or lower index (compared to the average of 100) is the relative *magnitude* of difference from the average. For example, an index of 175 (75 percent greater than average) has a greater magnitude of difference from the average than an index of 150 (50 percent greater than average).

The calculation to determine all indices is the same for all numbers, whether they are average, above average, or below average. For example, the index for females aged 12 to 17 is 61: 6.1 (percent) divided by 10.0 (percent) = 61 (percent). The 61 index has a *negative magnitude* of difference from the average of 39 percent:

10.0% of population − 6.1% of users =

3.9 percentage points difference = 39% difference (3.9—10.0)

As shown in Table 15.1, it is valid to say that females 25 to 34 are the primary *target*. Index alone, however, should not necessarily be the only factor in determining target groups. Consider, for example, that females 35 to 49 and 50+ each account for substantially more total users (5.0 million and 4.9 million, respectively). By targeting only females 25 to 34, and assuming you are able to purchase media to reach only this age segment, you would be missing a substantial portion of Product X users.

An alternative method to calculating an index is to use the *coverage* within each age cell compared to the national average coverage. In Table 15.2, the users are taken as a percent of each age cell, rather than as a percent of total U.S. users—e.g., of the females aged 12 to 17, 9.2 percent used Product X compared to 15.0 percent of all females aged 12 and older:

9.2 (percent) divided by 15.0 (percent) = 61 (percent) index

The concept of index can be applied to any two sets of numbers. In the previous examples, we compared users and population. In Table 15.3 we display media delivery. Shown are three media entities, their ratings among men, and the index of rating by geographic area.

Table 15.2. Calculating an Index (Alternative)

	Population		Product X Users		
	Number (in millions)	**% Total**	**Number (in millions)**	**% Total (across)**	**Index**
12–17	12.0	100.0	1.1	9.2	61
18–24	14.4	100.0	2.5	17.4	116
25–34	24.0	100.0	4.5	18.8	125
35–49	33.6	100.0	5.0	14.9	99
50+	36.0	100.0	4.9	13.6	91
Total	120.0	100.0	18.0	15.0	100

Table 15.3. Using Index Tto Compare Media Delivery Concentrations

	TV Program A		Radio Program B		Magazine C	
	Rating	Index	Rating	Index	Rating	Index
Northeast	9.2	115	1.1	92	1.4	74
East Central	7.2	90	1.3	108	2.0	105
West Central	9.2	115	1.3	108	2.0	105
South	8.8	110	1.5	125	2.0	105
Pacific	6.0	75	.9	75	2.2	116
Average	8.0	100	1.2	100	1.9	100

We see distinctly different delivery patterns, e.g., TV Program A is relatively stronger in the Northeast and West Central areas, while Radio Program B is strongest in the South, and Magazine C has its greatest relative strength in the Pacific area.

Brand Development Index

Indices are used to express any relationship of numbers within any category. Commonly, a brand development index (BDI) is displayed by geographic area to show how each area is performing relative to the average U.S. performance. As shown in Table 15.4, Markets A and D are above average, Market B on average, and Markets C and E below average.

The indices in Table 15.4 could be calculated in various ways and still yield the same conclusions. Method 1 is to divide the percent of total sales accounted for in each market by the percentage of total population in that market:

$$\text{Market A}$$

$$\frac{\%\ \text{Brand sales}}{\%\ \text{Population}} = \frac{11}{10} = 110\ \text{BDI}$$

Method 2 is to divide the share of market in each area by the average U.S. share of market. In this example, the brand commands a 22 percent share of market in Market A—i.e., of all the product category sold in this market, this particular brand accounts for 22 percent of the total. The average market has a 20 percent share. Therefore:

$$\text{Market A}$$

$$\frac{\%\ \text{of Market A}}{\%\ \text{Average market}} = \frac{22}{20} = 110\ \text{BDI}$$

Table 15.4. Brand Development Index

Market	% U.S. Population	% Brand Sales	BDI	Share of Market	BDI
A	10	11	110	22	110
B	15	15	100	20	100
C	20	18	90	18	90
D	25	30	120	24	120
E	30	26	87	17	87
Total	100	100	100	20	100

Category Development Index

A category development index (CDI) is identical in concept and arithmetic to a BDI, but it addresses category sales instead of product sales. The usefulness of CDI is either to define pockets of strength or weakness for a category when, for example, you have a new product entering the market, or to assess brand development vis-à-vis category development. Table 15.5 shows that this brand has strength in Market A (110 BDI), but is slightly underdeveloped when compared to the category (120 CDI).

The last column on the table is an index that compares BDI to CDI. Doing this exercise allows the planner to quickly and superficially detect areas of strength/weakness, such as market A, which has a lower BDI than CDI (i.e., a 92 index).

Table 15.5 BDI Compared to CDI

Market	% Population	% Sales Category	% Sales Brand	Index (% Sales/% Population) Category	Index (% Sales/% Population) Brand	Index (BDI/CDI)
A	10	12	11	120	110	92
B	15	15	15	100	100	100
C	20	16	18	80	90	89
D	25	30	30	120	120	100
E	30	27	26	90	87	103
Total	100	100	100	—	—	

16

Cost-per-Thousand (CPM)

CPM is an abbreviation of cost-per-thousand with the *thousand* from the Latin *mille*. It is the cost per 1 thousand individuals (or homes) delivered by a medium or media schedule.

CPM can be calculated for any medium, for any demographic group, and for any total cost. It conveniently shows the relative cost of one medium to another, or one media schedule to another. It is not unlike the cost per ounce found in supermarket pricing.

We use CPM to evaluate alternative selections—yet another method in determining the best medium or media schedule. For example, we might be considering the purchase of either Program A or Program B, weighing the price to be paid in terms of the audience each is delivering. By dividing the cost of each program by the delivery of each program, we can determine the cost-per-person:

Cost per program ÷ Number of people = Cost-per-person

$250 ÷ 50,000 = $.005

If we multiply the cost-per-person by 1,000, we arrive at a cost-per-thousand of $5.00. On a calculator, the faster method is to eliminate three zeros (1,000 people) from the number of people delivered by the program and perform the same division:

$250 ÷ 50 = $5.00

As shown in Table 16.1, the cost for a 30-second spot in Program A is $250. Program A delivers (is viewed by) 50,000 men and 25,000 women. The CPM for men is $5.00 and for women $10.00. Program B also delivers 50,000 men viewers but, because the cost for a 30-second spot is slightly higher, the CPM is $6.00. Conversely, Program B's CPM for women is less than that of Program A.

The second example shown in Table 16.1 is for magazines. Here we consider the purchase of a full-page four-color ad (1P4C). We find both costs and delivery for each magazine are different. By computing CPM for total men, we see both have the same *cost-efficiency* of $4.00. However, if the media plan's objective is to emphasize delivery to women, we find Magazine A is more cost-efficient: Magazine A delivers women at a lower CPM than Magazine B.

As a demonstration of how index can be used, Table 16.2 displays the CPM index for five magazine alternatives. Each magazine's CPM is compared to the average CPM of all magazines considered in this analysis. Note that the sum of all costs and deliveries are used to compute the $8.30 CPM average. Because each magazine has two variables (cost and audience), it is mathematically incorrect to add the respective CPMs and divide by five (which would result in a $9.92 CPM average).

Table 16.1. Calculating Cost-per-Thousand

	Cost for :30 Spot	Audience		Cost-per-Thousand	
		Men	Women	Men	Women
Program A	$250	50,000	25,000	$5.00	$10.00
Program B	$300	50,000	40,000	$6.00	$7.50
	1P4C*	Audience (in 1,000s)			
Magazine A	$50,000	12,500	8,000	$4.00	$6.25
Magazine B	$75,000	18,750	9,000	$4.00	$8.33

*Full-page, four-color ad.

Table 16.2. Calculating the Average CPM for Index Comparisons

Magazine	1P4-C*	Audience (in 1,000s)	CPM	Index
A	$50,000	8,000	$6.25	75
B	75,000	9,000	8.33	100
C	60,000	6,000	10.00	120
D	80,000	16,000	5.00	60
E	100,000	5,000	20.00	241
Total/Average	$365,000	44,000	$8.30	100

*Full-page, four-color ad.

17

Cost-per-Point (CPP)

The cost-per-point (i.e., cost-per-rating point) is the cost of purchasing one rating point. The term usually applies only to electronic media: television and radio.

The primary function of a CPP is to estimate the total cost of a planned TV or radio schedule within a market or nationally. For example, to determine how many TRPs are affordable within a given budget, divide the cost/TRP into the total budget. If your budget is $100,000 and you know that the CPP for the type of schedule you wish to buy is $250, you are able to purchase 400 TRPs:

$$\$100,000 \div \$250 = 400 \text{ TRPs}$$

Table 17.1 illustrates how CPP and cost-per-thousand (CPM) are related, though quite different from each other. The table shows a women population in Market X of 500,000. A 10-rated spot will therefore deliver 50,000 women. The cost for this 30 seconds is $250, resulting in a CPP of $25 and a CPM of $5. If you purchase 100 TRPs you deliver 500,000 impressions, i.e., the equivalent of the population. These 100 TRPs, at $25 CPP, will cost $2,500. Dividing the $2,500 by the 500,000 impressions results in a CPM of $5.

The formula for converting CPP to CPM, and vice versa, is:

$$\frac{\text{CPP} \times 100}{\text{Market population (in thousands)}} = \text{CPM}$$

$$\frac{\text{Market population (in thousands)} \times \text{CPM}}{100} = \text{CPP}$$

Table 17.1. Interrelationship of CPP and CPM

	Women	Cost	CPM
Cost/TRP		$25	
10 Rating	50,000	$250	$5.00
100 TRPs	500,000	$2,500	$5.00
Population base	500,000		

The absolute cost-per-point for TV and radio is affected by many variables, such as market size and supply and demand. Generally, the larger the market the higher the CPP, although it is not necessarily a direct correlation. Generally, the greater the advertiser demand for commercial time in any particular time segment, the higher the CPP. Table 17.2 demonstrates CPPs for TV and radio in Market X for selected time segments. The index of cost is calculated in two ways:

1. For each medium relative to its own average.

2. For radio compared to TV.

Costs vary by market, by station within market, by the type of programming being purchased, and by season. The media planner should use the appropriate estimated CPP when considering all these variations. Table 17.3, for example, shows that the annual average CPP in Market X is $25. This varies through the year from a low of $20 to a high of $29, based on the demand and supply of TV advertising in

Table 17.2 CPP by Time Segment and by Medium in Market X

EST	Television :30		Radio :60		
	CPP	Index (down)	CPP	Index (down)	Index (across)
7–7:30 A.M.	$60	80	$40	160	67
1–2 P.M.	50	67	30	120	60
5–6 P.M.	60	80	35	140	58
8–9 P.M.	130	173	20	80	15
11–11:30 P.M.	110	147	20	80	18
1–2 A.M.	40	53	5	20	13
Average	$75	100	$25	100	33

Table 17.3. Estimating Affordable GRPs

	Cost/GRP	Affordable GRPs for $2,500	Cost for 100 GRPs
Annual average	$25	100	$2,500
Jan–Mar	$24	104	$2,400
Apr–Jun	$27	93	$2,700
Jul–Sep	$20	125	$2,000
Oct–Dec	$29	86	$2,900

each period. If the planner has a $2,500 budget on average, 100 GRPs can be purchased. This same budget spent in the July–September period will purchase 125 GRPs. Conversely, if the media plan calls for the purchase of 100 GRPs in this same period, the cost will be only $2,000.

While CPP is commonly used for electronic media, unit cost rather than CPP is used for print media. The reason for using unit cost for print or CPP for broadcast media has to do with the manner in which the media are planned. Print media is generally planned using specific magazines or newspapers, for which specific rates apply. Specific publications can be used with a high comfort level that an advertisement can always be purchased in that publication, i.e., print media can expand the number of pages of a given issue to accommodate increased advertising insertions. Broadcast media is generally planned on the basis of certain types of programs or time segments, but not necessarily specific programs. The number of commercial slots available in any particular program is limited. After these slots are sold to advertisers, there are no additional availabilities (avails). Further, Like print media, different programs have different unit rates. Not knowing which programs will have avails forces the planner to use average costs. These average costs come in the form of cost-per-point.

The pricing structure of out-of-home media (e.g., posters) is based on purchasing a package of locations that produces a certain level of gross rating points, referred to as *showings*. A #100 showing, for example, is equivalent to 100 GRPs. It is therefore not common to use the concept of CPP for out-of-home media.

.

18

Demography

Demography is the study of the characteristics of populations related to size, growth, density, distribution, and vital statistics.

Demographic analyses permeate marketing and media planning. Nearly all investigations of a brand's strengths and weaknesses, and a medium's strengths and weaknesses, involve a critical analysis of how people consume the product and "consume" media.

In order to make the right decisions in choosing specific media, the media planner must know who should be addressed in the media plan. The planner must also know to what extent different media deliver specific audiences—how many people of a particular population group view a television program, or read a magazine, or listen to a radio station, etc.

Demographic descriptions are available from many sources, not the least of which is the Bureau of the Census. The major syndicated media research companies (A. C. Nielsen, Arbitron, Simmons, MRI, etc.) all provide data on the basis of demographic "cells" (specified groupings of particular population groups, such as men 18 to 34, men in households with incomes of $20,000 to $25,000, etc.).

Although demographic studies are important to the planning process, they are usually considered of secondary importance to studies that define product *users*, or users of products within a given category. An assessment of product users is a more effective method of analysis because media selection is predicated on the ability to reach very specific groups of people who are most apt to purchase a particular product or service.

A product user study can therefore give the planner a more precise definition of each medium's ability to reach these users. A demographic study, in this context, is an inference. To say that men 18 to 34 years old have an above-average propensity to buy tennis shoes does not mean all these men have the same propensity. The inference is, however, that if you advertise tennis shoes to this group of men you have an above-average chance of reaching more of the men who actually do buy tennis shoes.

If user profiles are more useful than demographic profiles, the obvious question arises: Why aren't they used? There are four reasons:

1. Tradition. Demographic profiles have been used for many years as the standard practice for defining media objectives and selecting media.

2. The various sources do not all define users, or do not define users in the same manner. If all media cannot be analyzed on the basis of their ability to reach users of a specific product, then the analysis by definition will be incomplete.

3. The reported information in the syndicated research sources is based on a sampling of the population. The number of people in the sample reporting usage of a particular product might be so few as to make the data reported unreliable.

4. Not all products are reported by syndicated sources, nor all brands within a product category. New products, not on the market, of course, would not be reported until the products were purchased by consumers. This would make analysis impossible for those products not reported.

19

Psychographics/Clustering

It is increasingly more popular to describe consumers in multi-demographic terms, such as by combining gender, age, income, family size, etc. Instead of simply referring to a target audience as, for example, men 25 to 54, it is usual to describe a target as men 25 to 54 having a household income of $50,000 or more, who are married and have children under 18.

And as consumer and media research becomes more definitive in its reporting, it is also becoming increasingly more popular to go beyond basic demographics by analyzing *psychographics.* Psychographics is the description of people's lifestyle characteristics: Do they play tennis? How old is their house? Are they opinion leaders? and so forth. These lifestyle characteristics, and literally thousands of demographic descriptions gleaned from the U.S. Census, are combined by statisticians and then segmented into distinct *cluster* types. Each cluster uniquely describes demographics, attitudes, and purchase behavior. Often the clusters also describe media consumption patterns, or can be tied to syndicated media research to define the extent of a medium's usage within a cluster.

Six syndicated segmentation (cluster) systems are currently used by advertisers: Acorn, ClusterPLUS 2000, Micro Vision 50, and PRIZM are used for general marketing/advertising purposes; Cohorts and Niches are used primarily by direct-marketing companies to establish mailing lists. Although the data collection methods and the resulting description of a cluster vary from one syndicator to another, the general methods and reporting are similar. The description that follows is of ClusterPLUS 2000.

How Clusters Are Determined

Using the U.S. Census and related data, clusters are determined through a multivariate analysis of 1,600 demographic/life-style variables. As of this writing Strategic Mapping, Inc. has determined that there are 60 different "population groups," i.e., clusters, and that each person in the United States "fits" the basic description of one or another of these clusters. For example, if a person is (basically) in the top income group, middle aged, highly educated, married, and a white collar professional who lives in a prestige home in a suburban community, that person is described as being part of Cluster #1; an average-income person who is well educated, young, mobile, single, and lives in an apartment is part of Cluster #17; and so forth.

Assigning a person to a cluster is based on the theory that birds of a feather flock together: your neighbor is more likely to be "like" you than not. ClusterPLUS 2000 used blocks and ZIP +4s to describe neighborhoods. There are approximately 5 million blocks in the U.S. (as defined by the census), each composed of, on average, 30 households—about 75 people. The U.S. Census provides demographic data for each of these blocks. Therefore, if a given block has a demographic composition most like the demographic description of Cluster S03, all people living within that block are designated as being part of Cluster S03.

The geographic location of the block is not important. What is important is the demographic composition of the block. For example, people living within a certain block in Scarsdale, N.Y., could be identical (from a demographic composition point of view) to people living within the same kind of block in Kenilworth, Ill., or Beverly Hills, Calif. When thinking about clusters, keep two things in mind:

1. People within any given cluster group can be found throughout the United States. The number of people within a given cluster, however, varies from one geographic location to another. For example, Cluster S01 people (suburban, established, wealthy) tend to be more heavily concentrated in the Southwest and Northeast, while Cluster #17 people (average socioeconomic status) tend to be found in many geographic areas throughout the United States.

2. The essence of the ClusterPLUS 2000 segmentation suggests that it doesn't matter in which geographic location a person lives. The only important variable is the person's demographic and lifestyle pattern (which could be affected by the type of

geographic location: urban, suburban, rural), i.e., people in Scarsdale, Kenilworth, and Beverly Hills, who are part of Cluster SO1 are, for all intents and purposes, clones. Given the similarities in the demographic composition of these neighborhoods, there will be general similarities in their lifestyles.

People within Each Cluster

What can be found out about the people in each cluster? The first set of information that can be found is how many people are in each cluster and what their demographic/lifestyle pattern is. This includes many variables, such as the typical age, gender, household size, income, etc., as well as things like type of housing, number of years living in a particular geographic area, means of transportation to work, number of automobiles owned, and so forth. All of this information is based on U.S. Census data. Lifestyle and consumer behavior information are also included and are based on syndicated survey sources.

Because all of the above information is automatically collected on a block and block group basis, information can be tabulated by clusters within specified pieces of geography. ClusterPLUS 2000 composition, for example, is by ZIP code, county, Metro area, TV market, state, and region.

ClusterPLUS 2000 can also be tied to other databases, such as MRI, Nielsen, Simmons, etc., to determine specific product and media consumption patterns. MRI and Simmons study the product/service consumption patterns and leisure activity patterns for hundreds of items: from beer to frozen yogurt to credit cards to propensity to play tennis, etc. Therefore, with ClusterPLUS 2000 tied to these research surveys, the number of people within each cluster who consume a certain product or perform a certain activity can be estimated.

Audience Data and the Cluster

All media audience data is based on a sampling of people. The address of each person in the sample is known by the research company doing the audience survey. These addresses are geographically coded (geo-coding) and designated by block and ZIP +4. Knowing the block in which the survey respondent is contained allows automatic designation to one or another cluster group.

After all survey respondents' cluster descriptions are determined, ClusterPLUS 2000 literally adds up the number of respondents in each cluster who meet the target audience description. For example, assume that 10,000 people are surveyed for Product X consumption. Of the 1,000 people found to consume Product X, 100 are within Cluster SO5. This sampling is then projected to the entire population within the cluster to yield a total target audience population count. This target audience population is then compared to the total population within the cluster to yield the percent penetration of the target audience compared to the total population.

Selecting Key Clusters

Having user penetration for each of 60 clusters allows for the selection of those clusters that are "above average," i.e., those that display a relatively high concentration of the target audience. The concept behind selecting key clusters is identical to that of selecting key demographics (with the latter being the traditional method): to determine a precise focus against which media would be analyzed and selected.

A focus on adults 35 to 54 (traditional), for example, should provide more media delivery per dollar to this group than if media is purchased simply on the basis of household viewing. Likewise, a focus on adults 35 to 54 within key clusters should also enhance media delivery per dollar. The process of selecting key clusters is identical to that of selecting key demographics: starting with quantitative analysis, followed by judgment.

Combining Key Cluster Data with Media Consumption

Let us assume we have selected a dozen clusters as being key. We return to the basic premise: Whatever a Cluster SO1 person in Scarsdale does (in marketing terms), so do the Cluster SO1 people in Kenilworth, Beverly Hills, etc. This premise also applies to TV program preferences, radio format preferences, magazine preferences, etc.

Therefore, if we find that Program X and Program Y each get an 8.0 rating among adults 35 to 54, and Program X delivers a 12.0 rating among adults 35 to 54 in the 12 key clusters versus Program Y, which delivers a 6.0 rating to the same cluster groups, then Program X probably delivers more of the target audience than does Program Y.

20

Audience Composition

Audience composition is the percentage of individuals in each demographic cell.

Audience composition gives a clear indication of the concentration of audiences for each media vehicle. To this extent, it is not unlike the *reason* for calculating an index. The arithmetic, however, is different and much more straightforward. The inspection of audience composition data presupposes the question: "What amount of the total audience is my target audience?"

In Table 20.1 we see that two programs each deliver 50,000 viewers. Of the people who view Program A, 17,500 are men. These men represent 35 percent of all viewers (17.5 ÷ 50.0). Women account for 40 percent of the audience, teens for 15 percent, and children for 10 percent. Program B's audience composition is somewhat different, with proportionately more teens and children than men and women. It can be said that Program B s*kews* (is biased) toward younger audiences.

Table 20.1 Audience Composition

	Program A		Program B	
	Number (in 1,000s)	%	Number (in 1,000s)	%
Men	17.5	35	15.0	30
Women	20.0	40	12.5	25
Teens	7.5	15	12.5	25
Children	5.0	10	10.0	20
Total	50.0	100 %	50.0	100 %

Audience composition varies dramatically by media category as well as among the specific media vehicles within a category. It is not surprising to find that movies, as a program type on TV, have an audience composition similar to that of the population as a whole. Different movies, however, attract different audiences, and the audience composition for a specific movie could be markedly different from that of movies in general.

One should not make generalizations about the average audience composition of any media grouping. Each media vehicle should be assessed independently of the others.

Magazine Audiences

When we speak of magazine audiences, we generally mean total audience: The sum of all readers of a given issue regardless of how they received the magazine, where it was read, or to what extent it was read. There are different types of readers, who are generally grouped as follows:

1. **Primary readers**—Those readers in the household in which the magazine was purchased, regardless of whether they subscribe to the publication or purchase it at a store or newsstand, and regardless of whether they read it in their home or outside their home.

2. **Passalong readers**—Those readers not in the primary household, who might read the publication in their own home, at work, a barber shop, doctor's office, on an airplane, etc.

3. **In-home readers**—Primary or passalong readers who read the magazine in their own home.

4. **Out-of-home readers**—Primary or passalong readers who read the magazine outside of their home: at work, on airplanes, in doctors' offices, etc.

Various studies indicate a greater *value* for the in-home reader versus the out-of-home reader, and a greater value for the primary versus the passalong reader. The in-home and primary reader spends more time with the magazine and picks it up more often. This greater reading time and reading occasions give the reader a greater opportunity to be exposed to a specific advertisement. It is therefore not uncommon for the out-of-home reader or the passalong reader to be

Exhibit 21.1. Magazine Audiences

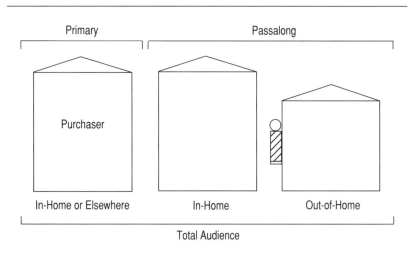

devalued by the planner whenever magazine audience data is reviewed and analyzed for CPM, etc. The value placed on in-home versus out-of-home readers must be fabricated by the planner—there is no golden rule. For example, if a planner decides the out-of-home reader is worth half as much as the in-home reader, the following arithmetic would apply: A magazine that has an audience of 1 million people, half of which are in--home and half out-of-home readers, would be considered by the planner as having 750,000 *weighted* readers:

	500,000 In-home readers	× 100%	=	500,000
+	500,000 Out-of-home readers	× 50%	=	250,000
	Weighted readers			750,000

Table 21.1 displays some general information on place of reading to give some understanding of these dynamics.

However, weighting audiences by place of reading or by method of receiving the publication should not be a sweeping decision applied to all publications. For example, *Inside Media* magazine is specifically edited for businesspeople involved with advertising media who generally read the magazine at their workplace, i.e., out-of-home. Also, in-flight publications reach a captive audience who appear to spend about as much time reading an issue as the average reader of a subscription/newsstand publication. *People* magazine, which has a relatively high percentage of out-of-home readers, commissioned a

Table 21.1. Where Adults Read Magazines

	Men	Women
Own home	60 %	63 %
Someone else's home	9	10
At work	12	10
Beauty parlor/barber shop	3	4
Doctor's/dentist's office	5	7
While traveling	3	1
All other locations	8	5
Total	100 %	100 %

Source: Magazine Dimension '94.

media research study to demonstrate that its out-of-home audience spends as much time reading the publication (i.e., has the opportunity to be exposed to the ads) as do its in-home readers because of the nature and layout of the magazine.

By way of comparison, note that other media also have in-home/out-of-home patterns, as shown in Table 21.2. Keep in mind that the patterns could change by market or by season. For example, in Los Angeles most people drive to work; in New York most people use public transportation to go to work. Method of commute affects out-of-home radio listening levels.

In addition to distribution channels affecting readership (i.e., how much of the circulation goes to doctor's offices, how much is single-copy versus subscription, etc.), patterns for in-home and out-of-home readership are also affected by the editorial emphasis of the magazine. For example, a high percentage of *Better Homes & Gardens* read-

Table 21.2. Location of Media Consumption

	Own Home	Someone Else's Home	Out of Home	Total
Magazines	62	10	28	100%
TV	92	4	4	100%
Radio	50	6	44	100%
Newspapers	86	2	12	100%
Outdoor	—	—	100	100%

Source: Magazine Dimensions '94.

ers read the magazine at home—a convenient place to think of home furnishings. *Business Week* readers are concentrated more out-of-home, most of them at work, which is a more convenient place to react to business information. *TV Guide,* used primarily as a television program listing, is obviously read mostly at home.

22

Readers-per-Copy

Readers-per-copy (RPC) is the total number of primary and passalong readers of a given issue of a publication. As a given issue of a publication is passed from one reader to the next, the number of readers of that copy increases, i.e., the readers-per-copy increase.

Many factors affect the number of readers-per-copy a magazine will garner. Among them are:

- **Distribution patterns.** Circulation in areas with a high potential audience, such as airplanes, doctors' offices, etc., allows more people to be exposed to a specific copy of a magazine. Much of this readership is passalong, and all is considered out-of-home reading.

- **Amount of editorial.** Physically, the more words contained in a magazine, the longer it takes to read. The primary reader will therefore hold that copy longer, with fewer passalong readers having the opportunity to see that issue.

- **Type of editorial.** Some publications have a tendency to be retained by the primary reader (not passed along) because of the reference material in the magazine, the reproduction quality, the "I'd like to keep this on my coffee table" syndrome, or any number of other reasons.

Readers-per-copy is determined by dividing the *total audience* of an average issue of a publication (as reported by various research companies) by the average issue circulation of that publication. It is not necessarily an accurate number,[1] but is commonly used by plan-

---

[1]First, total audience is an estimate based on a sampling of people. It is not an audit of every reader. Second, the audience estimate is usually based on a specific issue, while the circulation is based on a six-month average.

ners, and by advertising salespeople, to assess total audience dimensions. Similarly, an estimated RPC is often used for a new publication (which has not been surveyed for total audience) to determine its estimated total audience—for example, the average RPC for newsweeklies would be used to determine the total audience of a new newsweekly.

Table 22.1 displays the average RPC for magazines and newspapers. These are averages and not necessarily representative of a specific publication (nor of a specific publication at any particular point in time). These are estimates for the number of readers of a typical issue of a publication, regardless of how much of the publication, or which sections of the publication, were read.

Unlike electronic media, it takes time for a magazine to accumulate its total audience. A TV or radio program is short-lived. With the minor exception of people who record programs for later viewing or listening, electronic media deliver their audiences instantaneously. Print media are long-lived; the length of life is as long as it takes for the final passalong reader to read a specific issue. This amount of time varies by publication, depending on how long it takes the primary reader(s) to read an issue, pass it along, and then have succeeding readers do likewise.

Table 22.2 demonstrates the percent of total audience accumulated over time by various media forms. Accumulation patterns vary among specific publications. However, the general pattern is that weekly

Table 22.1. Readers-per-Copy

Type	Number of publications	Adults 18+	Men 18+	Women 18+
Magazines				
Business	7	4.64	3.21	1.43
General editorial	6	7.00	3.09	3.91
Men's	14	5.67	4.72	.95
Newsweekly	3	5.69	3.29	2.42
Women's	17	4.35	.55	3.80
Newspaper				
Weekday	—	2.28	1.17	1.11
Sunday	—	2.26	1.10	1.16

Source: MRI; Newspaper Association of America.

magazines accumulate their total audiences within five weeks; monthly magazines within 12 weeks; daily newspapers within (essentially) one day; newspaper supplements (i.e., in weekend editions) within (essentially) one week; TV within (essentially) one day; radio within one day; out-of-home media within four weeks.

These are some of the basic assumptions that researchers make when they assess magazine audience accumulation:

- The shorter the publication interval, the faster the accumulation.

- The higher the readers-per-copy, the slower the accumulation.

- Timely or news-oriented publications are consumed faster and therefore accumulate faster.

- The higher the percentage of newsstand circulation, the more rapidly the primary audience is accumulated.

- The larger the percentage of in-home audience a publication has, the faster its audience accumulation.

Table 22.2. Total Audience Accumulation Patterns

	Weekly Magazine	Monthly Magazine	Daily Paper	Supplement	TV	Radio	Out-of-Home
Same day	N/A.	N/A.	98	94	98	100 %	N/A.
Week 1	60	40	100%	98	100%		75
2	80	60		100%			85
3	90	72					95
4	98	79					100%
5	100%	84					
6		88					
7		91					
8		94					
9		96					
10		98					
11		99					
12		100%					

Source: MRI; Telmar; Author's estimates.

Audience accumulation varies by type of reader. The primary reader has the first opportunity to read a given issue of a magazine, and primary audiences are, therefore, accumulated faster. An independent research firm (SORTEM) conducted studies among primary and passalong readers that showed, for example, that among the four women's service magazines studied, 43 percent of the magazine's primary audience read the issues within the first week compared to only 15 percent of the magazines' passalong audience. Similarly, in-home audiences (which tend to have heavy concentrations of primary readers) are accumulated faster than out-of-home audiences.

23

Broadcast Dayparts

Broadcast dayparts are the time periods in a 24-hour day during which television and radio programs are broadcast.

Dayparts in TV and radio are used too by media planners as a starting point in deciding *where* advertising should be scheduled, to estimate how many TRPs might be affordable within a defined media budget (for which the cost-per-point by daypart is used), and for estimating reach/frequency.

Television has basically seven dayparts, shown in Table 23.1. The exact times vary by time zone and sometimes from market to market.

Table 23.1. Television Dayparts

	General Time Period (EST)	
Daytime	10:00 A.M.–4:30 P.M.	Monday–Friday
Early evening (or	4:30 P.M.–7:30 P.M.	Monday–Friday
early fringe)	5:00 P.M.–7:30 P.M.	Saturday & Sunday
Prime access	7:30 P.M.–8:00 P.M.	Monday–Sunday
Primetime (or	8:00 P.M.–11:00 P.M.	Monday–Saturday
nighttime)	7:00 P.M.–11:00 P.M.	Sunday
Late night (or	11:00 P.M.–1:00 A.M.	Sunday–Saturday
late fringe)		
Weekend children's	8:00 A.M.–2:00 P.M.	Saturday & Sunday
Weekend afternoon	2:00 P.M.–5:00 P.M.	Saturday & Sunday
(including sports)		

Exhibit 23.1. Audience Composition by Daypart

	Daytime	Early Evening	Prime Access	Prime	Late Night	Weekend Children's	Weekend Afternoon
Women (18+)	55	44	45	45	47	26	38
Men (18+)						23	
Teens (12–17)	21	35	35	37	42	14	42
	8	8	7	8	6	37	9
Children (2–11)	16	13	13	10	3		14

Source: A.C. Nielsen.

As shown in Exhibit 23.1, each daypart attracts different audiences because of the programs being telecast as well as the availability of viewers. Men are less available during the daytime TV hours; therefore, women account for the lion's share of viewers. This fact remains true despite the increase of working women, who are less available to view daytime TV. Late night TV programming attracts adult viewers, the majority of them young adults. Saturday morning programs are viewed primarily by children, whereas programs telecast during weekend afternoons attract proportionately high levels of men viewers.

As stated in Chapter 20, "Audience Composition," generalities can be misleading. There are wide variations in the demographic composition of the viewers by program within dayparts.

Exhibit 23.2 displays audience composition for primetime TV comparing the average of all programs to three specific shows. If you purchased many different programs in primetime (a high dispersion schedule), odds are you would achieve a distribution of impressions as shown for primetime. Selecting specific programs, however, could substantially alter the distribution, e.g., nearly 100 percent of impressions would be accounted for by adults if "Seinfeld" was purchased; 47 percent of impressions would be accounted for by teenagers and children if "Simpsons" was purchased.

Radio has essentially five dayparts (see Table 23.2). Planners sometimes also refer to a sixth daypart, Weekend, which encompasses the 24 hours of Saturday and Sunday.

Exhibit 23.2. Audience Composition Variations in Primetime

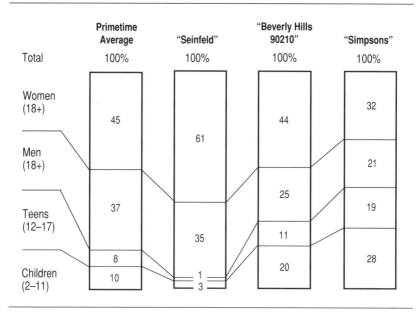

	Primetime Average	"Seinfeld"	"Beverly Hills 90210"	"Simpsons"
Total	100%	100%	100%	100%
Women (18+)	45	61	44	32
Men (18+)	37		25	21
Teens (12–17)		35	11	19
Children (2–11)	8 / 10	1 / 3	20	28

Source: A. C. Nielsen.

Table 23.2. Radio Dayparts

Common Reference	General Time Period
Morning drive (A.M. drive, primetime)	6:00 A.M.–10:00 A.M.
Daytime	10:00 A.M.–3:00 P.M.
Afternoon drive (P.M. drive, primetime)	3:00 P.M.–7:00 P.M.
Nighttime (evening)	7:00 P.M.–midnight
Overnight	Midnight–6:00 A.M.

Unlike television, audience composition by daypart varies only slightly (see Table 23.3). Composition by programming type (format), however, shows marked differences (see Table 23.4).

Table 23.3. Audience Composition by Radio Daypart

Daypart	Teens 12–17	Men 18+	Women 18+	Total
Morning drive	11	43	46	100%
Daytime	10	42	48	100%
Afternoon drive	11	41	48	100%
Evening	12	35	53	100%
Overnight	11	39	50	100%

Source: Radio Advertising Bureau.

Table 23.4. Audience Composition by Radio Format

Format	Teens 12–17	Adults 18–34	Adults 35–54	Adults 55+	Total
Adult contemporary	4	45	37	14	100%
Album-oriented rock	9	78	12	1	100%
Big band	*	5	17	78	100%
Black	7	39	32	22	100%
Classical	1	15	40	44	100%
Classic hits	3	62	29	6	100%
Classic rock	5	73	21	1	100%
Contemporary hit rock	26	54	17	3	100%
Country	2	24	41	33	100%
Easy listening	1	10	32	57	100%
Golden oldies	3	35	51	11	100%
Jazz	1	41	48	10	100%
Middle of the road	1	11	30	58	100%
All news	1	13	31	55	100%
News/talk	*	12	28	60	100%
New wave	16	67	16	1	100%
Religion	1	19	28	52	100%
Soft contemporary	3	46	40	11	100%
Spanish	5	37	34	24	100%
All talk	*	10	25	65	100%
Urban contemporary	17	52	23	8	100%

*Less than 1 percent.

Source: Bob Schulberg, Radio Advertising, *The Authoritative Handbook*.

24

Geographic Areas

Most source material showing product sales or media delivery presents information on some territorial basis that allows the media planner to make evaluations based on geographical units rather than relying only on national data. This type of investigation leads to more precise media plans—plans that target not only demographic groups, but demographic groups within specific cities, states, etc. Here are the more common geographic units.

Broadcast Coverage Area

A broadcast coverage area is the geographic area within which a signal from an originating television station can be received.

Exhibit 24.1. Broadcast Coverage Area

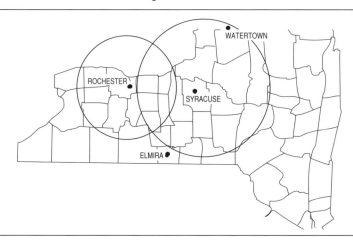

A television signal is broadcast from a point of origin. As shown in Exhibit 24.1, TV stations originating in Syracuse, N.Y., can be viewed in an area extending from Watertown down to Elmira. People living in Yates County are within the broadcast coverage area of both Syracuse and Rochester stations (Exhibit 24.2).

Television Market

A television market is an *unduplicated* geographic area to which a county is assigned on the basis of the highest share of viewing of originating stations.

A. C. Nielsen surveys viewing habits in every county in the United States. This data reports how much the people in each county view each TV station. With this data, we are able to determine which stations are viewed most and then assign the county to one market or another.

The homes in Yates County (see Exhibit 24.2) view more hours of programs originating from Syracuse than they do programs coming from Rochester stations. Yates County, therefore, is assigned to the Syracuse television market.

It is necessary to place a county in only one TV market to avoid an overlap of information. If a county were assigned to more than one television market, it would make geographic analyses of media delivery impossible.

There are 211 TV markets in the United States; these markets encompass more than 3,000 counties. Arbitron's term for a TV market

Exhibit 24.2. Television Market

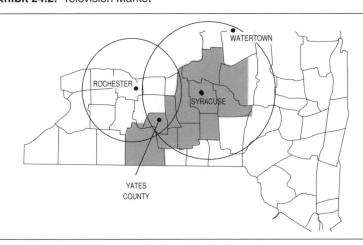

was Area of Dominant Influence (ADI); Nielsen's term is Designated Market Area (DMA). Although the terms differ, and to some extent so do the research techniques establishing viewing habits, ADI and DMA are quite similar, and both are synonymous with the term "TV market."

Metropolitan Statistical Area

Designated by the federal Office of Management and Budget, a Metropolitan Statistical Area (MSA) always includes a *city* (or cities) of specified population, which constitutes the central city, and the *county* (or counties) in which it is located. An MSA also includes contiguous counties when the economic and social relationships between the central and contiguous counties meet specified criteria.

The basic criteria for an MSA are:

- It must include at least one city with 50,000 or more inhabitants, or an urbanized area of at least 50,000 inhabitants and a total Metro area population of 100,000 or more.

- It must have one or more central counties. These are the counties in which at least one-half the population lives in the Census Bureau urbanized area.

Counties that do not meet the above criteria could be included in an MSA if they satisfy other requirements. There must be significant levels of commuting from the outlying county to the central county (ies), and the county (ies) must display a specified degree of "metropolitan character" by meeting any one of the following conditions:

- Counties with a commuting rate of 50 percent or more must have a population density of at least 25 persons per square mile.

- Counties with a commuting rate from 40 to 50 percent must have a population density of at least 35 persons per square mile.

- Those with a commuting rate from 25 to 40 percent must have a population density of at least 50 persons per square mile, or at least 35 percent of their population classified as urban by the Bureau of the Census.

- Counties with a commuting rate from 15 to 25 percent must have a population density of at least 50 persons per square mile, and meet two of the following requirements:

  - Population density must be at least 60 persons per square mile.

  - At least 35 percent of the population must be classified as urban.

  - Population growth between 1980 and 1990 must be at least 20 percent.

  - Either 10 percent or at least 5,000 persons must live within the urbanized area.

In addition to the designation of MSAs, the government has also defined two other geographic entities.

1. Consolidated Metropolitan Statistical Area (CMSA). This is the largest designation in terms of geographic area and market size. It is made up of component PMSAs. These CMSAs, or *mega* areas, are usually of little use to marketers because of their prohibitive size. However, they exert some influence on bordering counties because of the proximity of potential buyers for area goods and services.

2. Primary Metropolitan Statistical Area (PMSA). These are the component pieces that make up the CMSAs. They are directly associated with other PMSAs, but remain separate entities in terms of the socioeconomic data collected for them and presented in various research reports. To be classified as a PMSA, an area must be comprised of counties that conform to the following standards:

- A total population of at least 1,000,000.

- A population that is at least 60 percent urban.

- Less than 50 percent of the resident workers commute to jobs outside the county (ies).

Total Survey Area (TSA)

This term is used for radio. It is an *area,* but in the traditional sense not a market.

A TSA is composed of counties in which radio stations from an originating market have *coverage*. For a county to be part of a TSA, people living in the county must have established certain levels of listening to the radio station(s) broadcasting within their geographic area. These listening levels are tabulated from the survey diaries filled out by those in the survey sample. One listening level, for example, requires that a radio station be mentioned (listed) in at least ten diaries as being listened to for at least five minutes during any quarter hour within a survey week.

TSAs can overlap; a county can be part of more than one TSA. The Los Angeles–Long Beach Metro Area is composed of the counties of Los Angeles and Orange. The Los Angeles TSA extends well beyond these two counties to include the counties of Inyo to the north, Santa Barbara to the northwest, and San Diego to the south. San Diego county is also part of the San Diego TSA. Because TSAs overlap, it impairs any geographic media analysis. For example, should product sales and population in San Diego county be attributed to Los Angeles or San Diego? Additionally, these somewhat amorphous pieces of geography are not studied by syndicated research companies (with the exception of Arbitron, which studies radio listening), which makes geographic analysis myopic.

As stated in Chapter 10, "Reach/Frequency/GRPs," it is important to analyze media delivery for the TSA, not just the MSA. This is especially important for advertisers who do not have specific geographic boundaries in which they want to restrict advertising delivery.

Newspaper Areas

The Audit Bureau of Circulation (ABC) verifies member newspapers' total circulation statements and reports circulation on various geographic bases that aid the media planner in assessing precisely where the newspaper is distributed. Three geographic units are generally reported:

- **City Zone** is the area bounded by the corporate limits of the community in which a newspaper is published. Additional contiguous areas are included in the City Zone if these areas have the same characteristics as the community itself.

- **Retail Trading Zone** is the area beyond the City Zone whose residents regularly shop in the City Zone.

- **Newspaper Designated Market** is defined by the newspaper publisher and is that area in which the publisher believes the newspaper has its greatest strength on the basis of readership, editorial coverage of the communities, and advertising.

Nielsen County Size Groups

Nielsen County Size Groups are composed of counties assigned to one of four designations by A. C. Nielsen, based on population density and labor force concentration.

The specific definition of each county size group is as follows:

A   All counties belonging to the 21 largest MSAs, from the 1990 Census (see Table 24.1).

B   All counties not included under "A" that have more than 85,000 households.

C   All counties not included under "A" or "B" that either have more than 20,000 households or are in metropolitan areas of more than 20,000 households.

D   All remaining counties.

County size is used to investigate urban/rural patterns of sales and media delivery. Several syndicated sources show sales as well as media delivery (such as magazine circulation) on a county-size basis. Quick assessments can be made about the concentrations in the biggest cities ("A"), big cities ("B"), smaller cities ("C"), and rural areas ("D"). If sales for Product X skew to "A" counties and Magazine Y has its highest penetration in "C" and "D" counties, then Magazine Y is probably not a desirable medium.

County-size investigations should be made as an adjunct to TV market analysis or in lieu of TV market data when the latter is not

Table 24.1. MSAs Comprising County Size Group "A"

Atlanta	Houston	Pittsburgh
Baltimore	Los Angeles	San Diego
Boston	Miami	San Francisco
Chicago	Minneapolis/St. Paul	Seattle/Tacoma
Cleveland	New York	St. Louis
Dallas/Fort Worth	Philadelphia	Tampa/St. Petersburg
Detroit	Phoenix	Washington, D.C.

available. For example, if we are estimating potential sales for TV markets for which there is little or no sales data available, we can assume that counties within the TV market will perform by size as do the national sales by county size.

Many syndicated research sources delineate population, product category sales, and media delivery by TV market (DMA) and by Metro area, which makes geographic analysis convenient. When analyzing this data, or when devising a list of markets that should receive media delivery attention for one or another reason, the planner should keep the following in mind:

- The Metro area is the hub of a TV market, but does not encompass the entire population of the TV market. With more than 300 Metro areas and approximately 200 DMAs, the average TV market contains 1.5 Metro areas. It would be misleading to tally only Metro area data to decide TV market selection.

- Ranking Metro areas or DMAs should be done on the demographic basis to which the media delivery will be focused. It would be incorrect, for example, to select the top ten DMAs based on TV households if the media plan is directed to Hispanics.

Tables 24.2 and 24.3 show the "Top Ten" markets—first for DMAs and then for Metro areas. You will note that the ranking of markets based on Hispanic population or Black population is distinct from that of the overall ranking (i.e., the TV households or total households ranking). Harlingen, for example, is the eighth largest Hispanic DMA, but ranks 115th based on TV households. You will also note in these tables that Metro areas are quite different from DMAs, often in name and always in terms of population. For example, the Los Angeles DMA is split apart on a Metro-area basis and includes the Metros of Los Angeles/Long Beach, Riverside/San Bernardino, and Orange County. The New York DMA contains nearly 3 million Hispanics, while the New York Metro area has just under 2 million.

Table 24.2. Ranking of DMAs

Top Ten DMAs Based on TV Households		Number (in 1,000s)	Hispanic Population		Black Population	
	Rank	Number (in 1,000s)	Rank	Number (in 1,000s)	Rank	Number (in 1,000s)
New York	1	6,692	2	2,973	1	3,746
Los Angeles	2	5,006	1	5,080	3	1,309
Chicago	3	3,071	4	989	2	1,647
Philadelphia	4	2,661	—	320	4	1,252
San Francisco/ Oakland	5	2,253	5	975	—	533
Boston	6	2,105	—	260	—	299
Washington	7	1,855	—	269	5	1,183
Dallas/Ft. Worth	8	1,817	9	657	9	681
Detroit	9	1,735	—	96	6	1,013
Houston	10	1,511	6	942	8	789
Additional DMAs						
Atlanta	11	1,510	—	82	7	991
Miami/Ft. Lauderdale	16	1,297	3	1,202	10	669
San Antonio	40	611	7	892	—	109
Fresno	57	473	10	570	—	71
Harlingen/Weslaco/ Brownsville/McAllen	115	203	8	678	—	2

Source: SRDS Newspaper Advertising Source; SRDS Television and Cable Source.

Table 24.3. Ranking of Metro Areas

	Top Ten Metro Areas Based on Total Households		Hispanic Population		Black Population	
	Rank	Number (in 1,000s)	Rank	Number (in 1,000s)	Rank	Number (in 1,000s)
Los Angeles/ Long Beach	1	9,306	1	3,748	4	1,091
New York	2	8,643	2	1,982	1	2,587
Chicago	3	7,663	4	929	2	1,497
Boston/Worcester/ Lawrence/Lowell/ Brockton	4	5,773	—	269	—	304
Philadelphia	5	5,015	—	191	5	985
Washington	6	4,471	—	264	3	1,148
Detroit	7	4,313	—	89	6	978
Houston	8	3,568	6	820	8	679
Atlanta	9	3,278	—	70	7	848
Riverside/ San Bernardino	10	3,024	5	864	—	232
Additional Metro Areas						
Dallas	11	2,901	—	441	10	470
San Diego	13	2,694	9	589	—	187
Orange County	15	2,600	8	663	—	52
Baltimore	17	2,461	—	33	9	642
Miami	24	2,015	3	1,062	—	440
San Antonio	38	1,424	7	698	—	100
El Paso	76	649	10	471	—	25

Source: SRDS Newspaper Advertising Source; SRDS Television and Cable Source.

25

Major Media Forms

The average person is exposed to hundreds (perhaps thousands) of advertising messages each day. These messages include commercials on TV and radio; tune-in promotional announcements; sponsorship mentions on TV and radio; ads in magazines and newspapers; ads on outdoor posters and posters in sports arenas; ads in and on buses, trains, taxis, and trolleys, and at bus stops and train stations; point-of-purchase placards and posters in store windows, on supermarket shopping carts, and suspended from aisles and shelves; ads on matchbook covers; skywriting on earth's side of the sky and airplane tows; audible or visual product mentions in theatrical and made-for-TV movies; and the list could go on and on. There are hundreds of distinctly different media vehicles in which, and on which, advertisers can place advertising messages.

This chapter does not intend to provide the media planner with a complete list of media offerings. The list would encompass a complete book. The intent is to explain the basic structure and some of the advertising offerings of the major media forms. Some refer to these media forms as traditional, standard, or mass media. For the most part, specific traditional media are known by their geographic concentration: national, regional, local, as shown in Table 25.1. The discussion covers each of these media forms. A brief discussion on new electronic media, referred to by some as *interactive media* is included.

Network TV (Broadcast)

A network is any group of local television stations electronically joined to broadcast the same programs, usually simultaneously. Generally, a

113

Table 25.1. Basic Advertising Offerings of Major Media Forms

	National	Local/Regional
Electronic	Network TV	Regional network TV
	Syndication	Spot TV
	Network cable TV	Unwired spot TV
	Network radio	Spot cable TV
	Syndication radio	Spot radio
		Unwired spot radio
Print	Magazines	Magazines
	Newspapers	Newspapers
	Newspaper-distributed magazines	Newspaper-distributed magazines
		Out-of-home

network broadcasts its programming and the commercials contained in the programs nationally, i.e., on at least one local station in each TV market in the United States with which the network has an agreement to carry its programs. The network sells commercial time in its programs.

There are four TV broadcast networks (ABC, CBS, Fox, NBC) and two Hispanic broadcast networks (Telemundo and Univision).[1] The stations affiliated with these networks (some of which are owned by the networks) contract to air a certain amount of network programming each week—usually about 100 hours. In return, the stations are paid a compensation or fee. The reason the network pays the station is because the station is giving the network *time segments*—segments in which the local station could broadcast its own programming and, most importantly, in which it can sell commercial time. The local station is therefore giving up advertising revenue it might be able to receive in lieu of having *network programming* air in its local market. Local stations accept this trade-off on the basis that:

1. They are saving production expenses by not creating and producing their own local programming; and

2. They believe the quality of network programming and the advertising/promotion a network does to attract viewers to its

---

[1]As of this writing United Artists/Paramount and Warner Brothers have separately announced plans to create an additional network that will bring the total number of broadcast networks to five.

programs will give the local station prestige that will increase viewership of its local programming.

When networks first emerged they were called *Webs* because the visual representation of programming originating in New York and carried by many stations throughout the United States reminded one of a spider's web. The reference changed to *Line* networks when all programming was transmitted via telephone lines. Today, network programming (and commercials) are primarily transmitted from any city (e.g., Los Angeles, New York) via satellite to any and all cities. This signal is received by a local TV station and then retransmitted— over the airwaves and via cable. The reference to *broadcast* indicates that the transmission signal can be received on a TV set over the air waves as opposed to reception coming from telephone or cable lines, or via a satellite dish. The only thing needed to receive broadcast TV is a TV antenna. However, if a person has cable TV, the broadcast program is received via cable rather than over the air waves.

For the most part, the local stations receiving the programming air it at the same time they receive it, or delay the broadcast due to time zone differences. For example, a program originating from New York at 9 P.M. (EST) is received in Chicago at 8 P.M. (Central Time) and aired locally at 8 P.M. The same program, received in Los Angeles (Western Time) at 6 P.M., is videotaped and broadcast at 9 P.M. local time. When a local station purposely delays a broadcast for reasons other than time zone differences, it is known as a *delayed broadcast,* or DB.

Commercial time on network TV can be purchased in a number of dayparts any day or night. The programming varies from one daypart to the next, from season to season, and, often in primetime, from week to week. On average, network programs account for two-thirds of all TV hours broadcast by a local (affiliated) station. The remaining one-third of the hours contain local programming. On *independent* (non-network–affiliated) stations, 100 percent of the program hours are accounted for by local or *syndicated* programming: news, movies, talk shows, etc.

Regional Network TV (Broadcast)

ABC, CBS, and NBC, although capable of transmitting their program-ming to all markets simultaneously, tend to transmit only to 6 to 7 cities scattered throughout the United States. Each of these cities is known as a *feed.* These cities receive the network signal via satellite and retransmit it to surrounding cities, i.e., they feed their surrounding geography. The major pieces of geography surrounding and including the feed point is known as a region.

The networks offer for sale commercial time in each of the regions to any advertisers wishing to purchase it. The regional availabilities are far fewer than national avails. The networks clearly would rather sell their entire lineup of stations than to sell different pieces to different advertisers. Because all the regions combined equal total U.S. coverage, and because the networks want to receive advertising revenue for the sale of their complete U.S. offering, nearly every regional network buy requires a specific commercial slot be filled with a commercial in all regions. This is usually accomplished via the sale of commercial time to more than one advertiser, e.g., Advertiser A buys one-half of the regions and Advertiser B the other one-half. The mixing and matching of advertisers, regions, and commercial time in specific programs is a time-consuming process for the media buyer and media salesperson—yet another reason that limits regional network avails.

Syndication (Broadcast)

Syndication is a method of placing a program on a market-by-market basis as opposed to it airing "simultaneously" on a network. A syndicated program may be of any type and any duration. Some of these programs are original productions (which were either not secured by the networks for national airing or which the producer opted to be placed via syndication), and some are *off-network* programs, i.e., programs that originally aired on network TV and are replaying via syndication.

Placement on the local stations is usually contracted for by syndication companies who are involved with either the production of the program, or the local station placement, or both. There are various financial scenarios involved in these agreements. One scenario involves the syndicator retaining ownership of some of the commercial slots in the program and giving the program to the local station gratis. The syndicator sells these retained slots to national advertisers, and the remaining slots are sold on a local market basis.

The number of stations (markets) that agree to carry the program varies from one program to another (but not from one episode of the program to another). Adding the percent of U.S. TV homes in each market carrying the program constitutes the syndicated program's *clearance*. For example, a program airing in 150 markets that, combined, equal 80 percent of U.S. TV homes has a clearance of 80 percent. Network TV programs, by and large, have 95 percent or greater clearance.

Syndicated programs can air on network-affiliated or independent stations. When airing on network affiliates, the air time is during nonnetwork programming air times. Because each local placement is separately contracted, the local air time (and often the day of the week) a syndicated program will air varies from market-to-market.

Commercials can be placed in a syndicated program, depending on availability, in one of two ways:

1. In all markets on the clearance list.

2. As a normal Spot TV purchase, market-by-market.

Spot TV (Broadcast)

Spot TV refers to the purchase of commercial time on a market-by-market, nonnetwork and nonsyndication basis. Spot TV can be purchased on either network-affiliated stations or independent stations. There are approximately 200 TV markets in the United States and 1,100 local TV stations.

As opposed to network buys, Spot TV purchases can be made on any station in any market. The number of markets purchased may range from one to all in the United States, and the number of spots can vary from one market to the next and from one station to the next. The geographic and local media delivery flexibility is one of the major reasons advertisers use Spot TV.

When spots are placed on affiliates, they usually air outside of network programming, i.e., on local origination programs or between network programs during a commercial break. In some cases, a Spot TV commercial could air within a network TV program when, for example, the network has unsold inventory that is turned back to the local stations for local sale.

An *unwired network* refers to the purchase of Spot TV in a number of preselected local markets with the list of markets tailored to the advertiser's need. Technically, buying time on an unwired network is not network TV, it's Spot TV. The term *unwired* was devised to distinguish this type of buy from true (what used to be telephone-line–connected) network TV. In effecting this type of buy, however, the media buyer deals with a national sales representative company (or two or more companies) that represents the selected stations in all the markets rather than dealing individually with each station's local sales representative.

Network Cable TV

Like broadcast networks, cable networks also transmit programming and commercials to local markets via satellite. The local cable operator (similar in concept to a local TV station) receives the signal via a satellite dish (earth station) and retransmits it to those households that subscribe to the cable service. Also retransmitted to subscribing households is the broadcast programming transmitted by the local TV station. Generally, a cable TV household receives all TV programming via cable, whether it is considered broadcast or cable programming.

There are basically three offerings to cable subscribers, two of which have no advertising commercials:

1. **Premium (pay) channels.** These include Cinemax, Disney, HBO, The Movie Channel, Playboy, and others.

2. **Pay per view.** Major boxing events and recently released theatrical movies, for example, are sold to subscribers for a one-time fee (payment for the one viewing).

3. **Basic cable.** To receive either premium channels or pay-per-view events, a household must subscribe to basic cable. Carried on basic cable channels are advertiser-supported and non–advertiser-supported network and local cable programs, and the network and local broadcast programs.

New cable networks come into existence more rapidly than broadcast networks. As of this writing there are four broadcast networks with Fox being the only new entry in recent years. The reason has to do with *channel capacity*. More cable channels than broadcast channels are available on which to transmit programming. The average market has 3 to 10 broadcast channels (VHF and UHF) and more than 40 cable channels (3 to 10 of which carry broadcast programming). A new broadcast network needs to either convince an independent TV station to affiliate with the network, or arrange for a station affiliated with a current network to change its affiliation. A new cable network can be placed on a currently unused cable channel.

Table 25.2 lists the advertiser-supported cable networks in existence as of this writing.

While broadcast networks have affiliated TV stations that carry their programming (and commercials), cable networks have agreements with local cable systems to carry their programming. Generally, the greater the number of systems that carry a network, the greater the number of TV homes able to receive that network and, in turn, the

Table 25.2. Advertiser-Supported Cable TV Networks

Network	Subscribing Households (in 1,000s)	% Penetration of all U.S. TV Households
A&E (Arts & Entertainment)	59,150	62
Americana Television Network	2,900	3
BET (Black Entertainment Network)	39,100	41
Cartoon Network	8,900	9
CMT (Country Music Television)	24,800	26
CNBC	51,500	54
CNN	63,925	67
Comedy Central	30,000	31
Discovery	62,965	66
E!	26,710	28
ESPN	63,920	67
ESPN 2	15,000	16
The Family Channel	59,400	62
Galavison	5,000 (1,600*)	5 (25*)
Headline News	51,400	54
Lifetime	60,100	63
MEU (Mind Extension University)	26,000	27
MTV (Music TV)	59,150	62
MTV Latino	1,600 (475*)	2 (7*)
Nick at Nite	61,055	64
Nostalgia Network	14,000	15
Sci-Fi	16,220	17
TBS (Atlanta†)	62,010	65
TLC (The Learning Channel)	30,530	32
TNN (The Nashville Network)	58,195	61
TNT (Turner Network Television)	62,010	65
Travel Channel	18,125	19
USA	62,965	66
VH-1 (Video Hits One)	49,610	52
Weather Channel	56,285	59
WGN (Chicago†)	39,000	41
WWOR (New York†)	13,500	14

*Among Hispanic households.
†Also known as *Superstations*. Only TBS positions itself as a network.

Source: Cabletelevision Advertising Bureau; A. C. Nielsen; SRDS Hispanic Media & Market Source.

greater the number of subscribers for that network. The subscription, however, is to the basic cable system, not to any individual network. More information on this follows in the section "Local Cable TV."

Regional Cable TV Networks

Regional cable TV networks are identical in concept and transmission technique to national cable TV networks, but restrict their programming transmission to selected geographic areas. Table 25.3 lists the advertiser-supported regional networks currently in existence.

Local Cable TV

Also called *Spot Cable,* local cable is to network cable what Spot TV is to broadcast network TV, albeit with some marked differences. There are approximately 11,000 local systems in the United States, each with a legally defined geographic coverage area. They are referred to as systems, not stations, because each transmits programming from multiple broadcast networks and stations and cable networks, and they can transmit their own local programming. Households that subscribe to cable receive all of their TV programming through the local cable system.

Local cable advertising can be purchased on almost all of the cable systems individually, or through an *interconnect* that combines separate systems in a given area. When these systems are connected electronically via microwave (known as a hard interconnect), the advertiser's commercial is telecast to all participating systems simultaneously. When participating systems are not connected electronically (known as a soft interconnect), the commercial is aired separately by each system (requiring either multiple dubs of the commercial to be given to each system, or *bicycling* a copy of the commercial from one system to another). Bicycling is a term used to signify the physical and sequential transfer of a videotape from one station to another, regardless of the method of transportation used for the transfer. Regardless of independent or interconnect status, local cable commercials can be received only by homes who subscribe to cable TV.

Commercials cannot be placed in broadcast programs that are retransmitted by the cable operators. If an advertiser purchases a commercial slot on broadcast network or Spot TV, the commercial will air in all homes tuned to that program, whether or not the home subscribes to cable TV. The local system operator can sell commercial

Table 25.3 Advertiser-Supported Regional Cable TV Networks

Regional Network	Primary Area	Subscribers (in 1,000s)
ASPN	AZ	400
Empire Sports Network	Buffalo, west/central NY	600
HSE (Home Sports Entertainment)	TX, LA, AK, OK, NM	4,000
HTS	MD, VA, DE, DC, NC, WV, PA	2,500
' KBL Sports Network	PA, OH, WV, MD, NY	2,000
MSG (Madison Square Garden Network)	NY, NJ, CT, PA	4,900
NEWSCHANNEL 8	VA, MD, DC	850
News 12 (Long Island)	Long Island, NY	650
NY1 News	New York City	1,300
OCN (Orange County NEWSCHANNEL)	Orange County, CA	512
PSN (Prime Sports Network)—		
Rocky Mountain	CO, WY, KS, NE, NM	1,200
PSN—Intermountain	UT, WY, MT, NV, ID	450
PSN—Midwest	IL, IN, KY, OH, MO, WI	280
PSN—Upper midwest	MN, IA, ND, SD, WI	300
PRIME Ticket Network	CA, AZ, NV, HI	4,200
PRIME Ticket La Cadena Deportiva	CA	1,500*
PRISM	PA, NJ, DE	400
PASS—Pro-Am Sports System	MI, OH	800
SportsChannel—Chicago	IL, IN, IA	2,300
SportsChannel—Cincinnati	OH, IN, KY, TN	1,400
SportsChannel—Florida	FL	1,600
SportsChannel—New England	CT, MA, NH, ME, VT, RI	1,500
SportsChannel—New York	NY	1,500
SportsChannel—Ohio	OH	1,400
SportsChannel—Pacific	CA	2,000
SportsChannel—Philadelphia	PA, NJ	1,900
SportsSouth Network	AL, TN, KY, MS, NC, SC, TN	3,700
Sunshine Network	FL	3,200

*300 among Hispanic households.

Source: Cabletelevision Advertising Bureau; SRDS Hispanic Media & Market.

time only in cable-originated programs (network, regional, or local). Unlike the broadcast networks, which control about two-thirds of an affiliated TV station's air time, cable networks control the majority, up to 100 percent of the air time, on the channel on which they appear. Also unlike network broadcast, cable network allows local systems to place local commercials (known as *local insertion*) in network programs. The number of local commercials in these network programs is controlled by the network. Any particular local cable system might have, for example, anywhere from zero to two or more minutes of commercial time per hour available for local sale, all depending on the agreements with the networks. Commercial time in programs that are locally originated (i.e., nonnetwork programs) is controlled by the local operator.

Whether network cable, regional cable, or local cable is purchased, the maximum percentage of homes able to receive cable-originated programming is a function of how many homes have cable TV. Table 25.4 lists the top 20 TV markets and the cable penetration in each. Also shown are the markets with the highest and lowest level of penetration.

Table 25.4. Cable Penetration by TV Market

U.S. TV Households Rank/TV Market	% Cable Penetration	U.S. TV Household Rank/ TV Market	% Cable Penetration
1. New York	64	14. Minneapolis/St. Paul	47
2. Los Angeles	59	15. Tampa/St. Petersburg	67
3. Chicago	55	16. Miami/Ft. Lauderdale	66
4. Philadelphia	71	17. Pittsburgh	75
5. San Francisco/Oakland	67	18. St. Louis	48
6. Boston	73	19. Sacramento/Stockton/Modesto	60
7. Washington	62	20. Phoenix	53
8. Dallas/Ft. Worth	49		
9. Detroit	62	Highest Penetration:	
10. Houston	51	165. Palm Springs	89
11. Atlanta	61	Lowest Penetration:	
12. Cleveland	63	80. Springfield, Mo.	46
13. Seattle/Tacoma	67	115. Harlingen/Westlaco/ Brownsville/McAllen	46

Source: A.C. Nielsen.

Network Radio/Syndication Radio

The basic concept and dynamics of network and syndicated radio are the same as network and syndicated broadcast TV. Radio networks and syndicators provide various types of programming to affiliated stations throughout the United States. The local stations receive compensation from the program supplier, either in the form of cash or through some trade (barter) arrangement, such as providing the station with marketing services.

Of the 9,900 commercial radio stations in the United States, nearly two out of three are part of a *wired network*. Until 1980 radio networks transmitted all programming (most of it newscasts) and commercials via telephone lines, hence the word "wired." Today, transmission is primarily via satellite. The amount of network programs carried by the local stations has substantially diminished, but the local stations now also carry network commercials within local programming.

More than 8,000 radio stations are either part of a wired network, or carry syndicated programming, or both. A host of syndicated programming is available to advertisers wishing national radio coverage. Syndicated programs, and commercials within these programs, are sent to local stations via reel-to-reel tape and compact discs (CDs).

Exhibit 25.1 lists the 46 networks currently in operation and Exhibit 25.2 provides a sample list of the many network and syndicated programs currently on-air.

Exhibit 25.1. National Radio Networks

ABC Radio Networks	Keystone Broadcasting Systems
American Sports Radio Network	Lotus Hispanic Radio Network
American Urban Radio Networks	Morningstar Radio Network
AP All News Radio	MRN Radio
AsiaOne Network	One on One Sports Radio Network
Associated Press Broadcast Services	Peoples Network
Beethoven Satellite Network	Premiere Radio Networks
Business Radio Network	Russian American Broadcasting
Cadena Radio Centro	Spanish Information Service
CBS Americas, Spanish Radio Network	Sun Radio Network
CBS Radio Network	Telemundo Radio Network
CBS Spectrum Radio Network	Trans-Net

continued

Exhibit 25.1. National Radio Networks (continued)

CNBC Business Radio	Tribune Radio Network
CNN Radio Network	UP Radio Network
CNN Radio Noticias	USA Radio Network
Concert Music Network	The Wall Street Journal Radio Network
CRN International	Westwood AC
EFM Media	Westwood CNN+
Global Satellite Network	Westwood Country
Hispanic Radio Network	Westwood Overnight
The Interep Radio Store Networks	Westwood Variety
Interstate Radio Network	Westwood Young Adult
Katz Radio Group Network	WOR Radio Network

Source: SRDS TV & Cable Advertising Source.

Exhibit 25.2. Some of the Many Network and Syndicated Radio Programs

Rush Limbaugh	John Madden
Howard Stern	Brent Musberger
Mark & Brian	Casey's (Kasem) Countdown
Don Imus	Rick Dees Weekly Top 40
G. Gordon Liddy	American Top 40—Shadoe Stevens
Dr. Joyce Brothers	Wall Street Journal Report
Bob Costas	Dow Jones Radio Network
Pete Rose	Premiere (Olympia) Sports Network
Paul Harvey	ESPN Sports Talk Network
Charles Osgood	Cla'ence Update of the Young & Restless
Peter Jennings	The Countdown—Walt Love

Spot Radio

Spot radio works in the same way as Spot TV. Local radio stations air local programming, such as news, music, etc. (or network or syndicated programming) and sell commercials within the local shows.

Likewise, unwired radio networks are identical to Spot TV in terms of how they are constructed and sold.

Just about every one of the nearly 10,000 local radio stations in the United States have programming that is categorized into one or another format. Chapter 23 on "Broadcast Dayparts" lists these formats.

Magazines

Magazines can be purchased nationally, regionally, or locally. The larger national magazines often offer opportunities for purchasing less than national circulation in predetermined geographic areas (for example, the Northeast, or the state of Florida, or the Chicago Metropolitan area). Additionally, many magazines circulate only in defined areas, such as *Sunset* on the West Coast, *Southern Living* in the Southeast, or innumerable local magazines designated only for specific cities.

Some publications offer demographic editions for purchase. An advertiser could buy space that runs only in copies directed to particular audiences (e.g., doctors only, businesspeople only, etc.) Some publications also offer the opportunity to customize circulation to predetermined ZIP code areas or *individuals*. In the case of individuals, the publications also offer the opportunity for the creative message (e.g., a one-page ad) to also include the person's name in the copy. Insertion of these individualized ads is referred to as *selective binding*. With all these types of demographic and customized editions, the circulation is restricted to only subscription, not newsstand, copies.

There are more than 2,000 consumer magazines that offer advertising space, as well as thousands of business/trade and agricultural/farm publications. For media planning convenience, consumer magazines are classified according to their editorial focus (as shown in Table 25.5). The designation into a classification, however, does not necessarily limit the publication to the editorial description. Indeed, many magazines can be placed in multiple classifications. For example, *Modern Maturity,* the largest circulation magazine in the United States, can be placed in both "general editorial" and "mature market."

In addition to purchasing ad space directly from the publication and having the advertisement printed by the publication, an advertiser can also purchase the space and supply the publication with a *preprinted insert* that is bound into the publication. A preprinted insert can be one or more pages, and it can be printed on paper stock not usually used by the publication for its typical edition. Some preprinted inserts contain a combination of editorial matter and advertising (with the advertising being for one or more advertisers) in order to separate advertisements from each other (as is often found in the typical magazine).

Table 25.5. Number of Consumer Magazines by Classification

Classification	Number	Classification	Number
Airline Inflight/Train Enroute	23	History	12
Almanacs & Directories	7	Home Service & Home	113
Art & Antiques	8	Horses, Riding & Breeding	34
Automotive	90	Hotel Inroom	12
Aviation	17	Labor, Trade Union	2
Babies	29	Literary, Book Reviews & Writing	11
Black/African-American	13	Mature Market	33
Boating & Yachting	47	Mechanics & Science	8
Bridal	15	Media/Personalities	1
Business & Finance	44	Men's	29
Campers, RVs, Motor Homes/Trailers	9	Metropolitan/Regional/State	212
Camping & Outdoor	16	Metro/Entertainment Radio/TV	12
Children's	1	Military & Naval	22
Civic	3	Motorcycle	27
College & Alumni	38	Music	57
Comics & Comic Techniques	6	Mystery, Adventure & Sci-Fi	8
Computers	29	Nature & Ecology	14
Crafts, Games, Hobbies & Models	113	Newsweeklies	14
Dancing	5	Newsweeklies (Alternative)	52
Disabilities	4	News-biweeklies, dailies, semi-monthlies	4
Dogs & Pets	23	Newsletters	10
Dressmaking & Needlework	7	Newspaper-Distributed Magazines	33
Editorialized/Classified Advertising	1	Parenthood	53
Education & Teacher	9	Photography	11
Entertainment Guides & Programs	34	Political & Social Topics	18
Entertainment & Performing Arts	26	Popular Culture	2
Epicurean	26	Religious & Denominational	38
Fishing & Hunting	111	Science/Technology	15
Fitness	11	Sex	3
Fraternal, Professional Groups	19	Society	4
Gaming	8	Sports	269
Gardening (Home)	19	Teen	27
Gay Publications	4	Travel	83
General Editorial	86	TV & Radio/Comm. & Electronics	19
Group Buying Opportunities	24	Women's	85
Health	45	Women's/Men's Fashions, Beauty	12
Hispanic	80	Youth	42

Source: SRDS Consumer Magazines & Agri-Media Source; SRDS Hispanic Media & Market Source.

Newspapers

Consumer newspapers are primarily local in distribution, though there are three national newspapers: *The Christian Science Monitor, The Wall Street Journal,* and *USA Today.*

Besides the commonly known daily newspaper, with editions in the morning, evening, throughout the day, and on weekends, there are also suburban weeklies (which are distributed in smaller towns or the suburbs or larger cities), college newspapers (distributed primarily at colleges and universities and college towns), as well as ethnic publications concentrating on the Afro-American market, Hispanic market, Asian market, etc.

Advertising in newspapers can be purchased in many ways, such as the typical black/white or color ad of almost any size positioned within any section of the newspaper at the publisher's discretion (called *ROP*—Run of Press), or within a preselected section (*Preferred Position*). Often, newspapers exact a higher price for specific positioning. With some exception, there is always space available on which to run an ad—unlike TV and radio, which have a limited supply of commercial inventory. The exceptions fall within the category of precise positioning, such as opposite the editorial page (*Op ed*), for which there is only one position available to all advertisers.

No TV or radio program or magazine is completely consumed by everyone who comprises the total audiences of the medium. For example, not every person who is considered a viewer of a TV program views every minute of that program. Likewise, not every newspaper reader reads every section (or every page of every section). In considering which sections might be best for a specific advertiser (based, for example, on the compatibility of the editorial and the creative mes-

Table 25.6. Number of U.S. Newspapers

Type	Number of Papers
Dailies (Mon–Fri/Sat)	1,611
Sunday edition	863
Suburban weeklies	3,041
College	1,692
Black	141
Hispanic	10
National	3

Source: SRDS Newspaper Advertising Source.

Table 25.7. Daily Newspaper Readership Patterns

Type of Reading/Section Read	Adults 18+	Men 18+	Women 18+
Generally read every page	57 %	58 %	55 %
Read some pages/sections	43	42	45
	100 %	100 %	100 %
Business/finance	74 %	77 %	72 %
Classified	73	75	72
Comics	74	74	73
Editorial	79	79	80
Entertainment	78	74	82
Food/cooking	73	66	81
General news	95	94	95
Home	72	68	77
Sports	75	84	65
TV/radio listings	73	72	74

Source: Simmons.

sage), the planner should keep in mind that, on average, specific section placement could reduce total audience reach (see Table 25.7).

Newspaper-Distributed Magazines

These are also known as Supps because they are a supplement to the Sunday or weekend editions of newspapers. There are three nationally syndicated supps (centrally edited and produced), which are distributed in local newspapers throughout the United States, and 30 locally edited and produced newspaper magazines (26 of which can be purchased either individually or as part of a national sales group (Sunday Magazine Network) (see Table 25.8).

Out-of-Home Media

Out-of-home media can be purchased almost everywhere in the United States, in any configuration of national, regional, or local placement. Indeed, out-of-home media are the most local of all general media forms inasmuch as one advertising unit can be purchased in one specific geographic location. Only direct mail could be considered more local.

Table 25.8. Newspaper-Distributed Magazines

Syndicated Supps	Number of Papers Carrying	Circulation (in 1,000s)
Parade	351	36,000
USA Weekend	406	18,000
Vista	36	775
Locally Edited Supps		
Total	30	17,000
Sunday Magazine Network	26	15,000

Source: SRDS Newspaper Advertising Source.

There are a vast number of out-of-home media availabilities ranging dramatically in form, size, and location (see Table 25.9). Two of the more popular varieties of *outdoor* are discussed here.

Posters (Poster Panels)

Poster advertising is preprinted, on paper or vinyl, and affixed to a permanent structure that is either freestanding or on a building wall. The most widely used posters are called *30-sheet* posters, which refers to the size but not the printing of the advertisement. Long ago the typical 30 sheet required 30 sheets of paper to print the advertisement. Technology has reduced this requirement to 10 to 18 pieces of paper, or one sheet of vinyl. The average 30 sheet measures approximately 11 feet by 23 feet.

The junior panel (sometimes called an 8-sheet or 6-sheet is about one-fourth the size of a 30 sheet and mechanically usually a direct

Table 25.9. Types of Out-of-Home Media

Common Reference	Examples
Outdoor	Posters, paints
Transit	Bus exteriors, bus interiors, rail/subway posters, bus/train station posters and clocks
In-store	Audio systems, shelf talkers, shopping cart cards/video, hanging aisle posters
Place-based	School bulletin boards, bike racks, health club videos, sports arena posters
Miscellaneous	Inflatable balloons, skywriting, in-movie theater (cinema), telephone enclosures

adaptation of a 30 sheet. The 3-sheet poster, however, is a vertical display, commonly measuring approximately 3 feet by 7 feet.

Painted Bulletins

These are outdoor advertising structures on which advertising is directly painted.

Paints are generally larger than posters, averaging a copy area of 14 feet by 48 feet. There are two varieties of painted bulletins:

1. **Permanent,** on which advertising remains fixed at one location for the duration of the purchase contract.

2. **Rotary,** in which the display face is physically moved to a new location within the market at stated intervals—usually every 30, 60, or 90 days.

Permanent paints are sold by the individual unit usually on a one-year basis. Most paints are given priority placement in a market and therefore generate higher levels of traffic (auto as well as pedestrian), as well as having greater visual impact than posters. This, combined with the fact that paints are more costly to produce, results in paints costing significantly more to purchase than posters.

Rotary painted bulletins can be purchased individually or in packages where all locations are changed periodically with no location being used more than once. This type of purchase depends on the availability in a market and/or the advertiser's requirement.

Showing

Posters and paints (and various other out-of-home media) are generally sold in combination in order to achieve a predetermined level of exposure within a market. These levels are expressed as *showings* of different size, such as #25 showing, #50 showing, etc. Showings are synonymous with gross rating points generated within one day. Therefore, a purchase of a #100 showing should achieve a *daily effective circulation* (DEC) equivalent to the population in the market in which the posters/paints are purchased. DEC refers to the number of people who are counted as having passed a particular panel, times the number of panels purchased. Because different panels produce different circulation levels, the number of panels comprising any particular size showing could vary from market to market and within market.

The planner should keep in mind that showing size refers to the total population in the market—similar in concept to buying household GRPs in television. A #100 showing, for example, does not necessarily produce 100 target rating points against any particular target audience. As was shown in the previous discussion on reach/frequency, outdoor media exposure varies by demographic group.

Interactive Media

This section of the book is out-of-date. It became out-of-date milliseconds after it was written. Technological advances in video, audio, and data transmission techniques are causing major changes in *how* consumers will receive advertising media, *what* consumers will receive, and how consumers will be able to *respond* to advertising messages.

With increasing speed, people are traveling on and in an electronic *information superhighway* where there is an integration of television, radio, computers, telephones, fax machines, and much more. Although as of this writing this highway is still being paved, it is believed that communication technology will make quantum leaps in the years ahead; the traditional media with which we are dealing today will be tomorrow's dinosaurs.

Digital compression and, to a degree, fiber optics, are the re-bars in the superhighway. Digitization reduces video, audio, and text to the computer language of binary code so that vast amounts of information can be transmitted via coaxial cable or fiber-optic cable. Coaxial cable is what is currently fed into cable subscribing homes. It's the same cable that is used to connect your VCR with your TV set. Coaxial cable is about $1/4$ inch in diameter. A strand of fiber-optic cable is pure glass no thicker than a human hair. With digitization and compression of the digitized signal, coaxial cable has the capacity to transmit one way (i.e., into the home) approximately 240 channels; 120 channels can be transmitted two ways. One strand of fiber-optic cable can transmit (one way) 80 channels and (two way) 40 channels. Therefore, about 2 to 3 strands of fiber-optic cable have the same channel capacity as $1/4$-inch-thick coaxial cable.

Fiber-optic cable is increasingly being used by cable operators for trunk lines primarily because it is more cost-effective to use than coaxial cable. A trunk line is the main line emanating from the cable operator's facilities from which branches (coaxial cable) are fed into individual homes. Coaxial cable is currently more cost-effective than fiber-optic cable for use from the trunk line into a home.

The average home in the United States now receives 30 to 40 channels (if it has cable TV). With the currently used analog technology, the average home *could* receive approximately 70 channels. By the year 2020 (or sooner) about 500 channels might be accessible. The increase in the number of channels will come as a result of digitized signals transmitted via fiber-optic cable. Access, however, assumes programming availability. If only 100 different programs are available (entertainment, information, on-line services, etc.), only 100 different channels are needed.

Combining these innovations with a TV set and a computer (wherein there is virtually no distinction between what is a TV and what is a computer), the average home not only will be able to receive transmissions, but also will be able to react to the transmission. Traditional media are basically one-way: the advertiser addressing the consumer. The new media will be two-way. Technology will allow a dialog between the advertiser and the consumer predicated, first, on the advertiser being able to address specific consumers (addressable media), and, second, on the consumer being able to directly and instantaneously respond to and manipulate what is being received. The response has to do with acceptance or refusal, such as clicking a "yes" button on the remote control to signify wanting to receive more information about an advertiser. The manipulation deals with the consumer's capability to alter what is being shown, such as changing camera angles on a sports event. This action-reaction is what we now term

Table 25.10. Penetration Levels of Various Electronic Devices and Media

Medium/Device	1995	2000	2041
TV set	98 %	99 %	100 %
Home computer	25	50	90
Home computer with CD-ROM	15	45	90
Home modem	15	30	80
On-line subscription	6	25	75
ACRT (All Communications Receiver/Transmitter)	—	5	48
Cable TV (wired or wireless)	65	72	100
VCR	80	90	100
DBS (Direct Broadcast Satellite)	*	15	*
Interactive capability	*	10	100
Holographic TV	—	—	27

*Less than 1 percent.

Source: 1995: Author's interpretation of data published by Times Mirror Company; Nielsen; CAB; Chicago Tribune; 2000/2041: Author's projections.

interactive media. In the not too distant future we will drop the adjective and refer to these new media forms simply as "media."

The following are some of the devices and media forms that might be termed "interactive." Currently, interactive advertising is being delivered via phone and mail, on CD-ROM, on-line services, and interactive kiosks. This list will expand as current technologies are honed and as new technological offshoots are developed.

- U.S. Mail and electronic mail

- The telephone

- Facsimile machine

- A computer with a modem

- Any advertising message with an 800 telephone number. TV/radio spots, infomercials, magazine/newspaper/outdoor ads, direct mail, etc.

- Magazine/newspaper ads with a reply coupon

- Home shopping by TV

- Home shopping by computer

- Interactive kiosks (e.g., in shopping malls)

- CD-ROM (entertainment, information, advertising)

- On-line services: AOL, CompuServe, Delphi, Genie, Prodigy, etc.

- Videogames

- Video cassette recorder/player

- Video on demand (VOD)

- Near video on demand (NVOD)

Interactive media currently are not a major media form—not in terms of what is available to consumers nor in terms of how many consumers are involved with or own interactive devices. There is, however, extraordinary interest among advertisers and media planners in these electronic media forms, far surpassing the interest in television as it developed in the 1940s and cable television since its early growth in the 1950s. The interest is more in the form of investigation than investment. Indeed, if advertisers spent $1 in interactive media for every word that has been printed on the subject, interactive media would account for a significant percentage of all advertising spending. Notwithstanding, as the penetration levels of interactive devices increase, the traditional media environment will fade. An ACRT (All communications receiver/transmitter) will replace today's TV, computer, CD, VCR, fax, and phone. Consumers will use an ACRT for all of their communication needs, and they will have total control on what is sent and, most important for advertisers, what is received.

Every major communications/entertainment company (telephone, computer, movie, broadcast, cable, radio, magazine, newspaper, videogame, and so forth) is involved in creating and/or testing the new technologies and attempting to get answers to the unknowns. The tests involve the obvious hardware and software, as well as programming and advertising applications. The programming (entertainment, information, shopping, etc.) consumers will want, how they will access that programming, and what they are willing to pay to receive that programming is not known. VOD (video on demand) or NVOD (near video on demand), for example, is desired by most people, but these same people have a limit as to how much they will pay for this service. Also not known is how advertising will be part of some of the program offerings, and what kind of advertising message will have to be created to be effective in an interactive environment. For example, because consumers will have an increased ability to choose programming and advertising, will they access a COD (commercial on demand)?

From a media-planning point of view, the biggest unknown is how to quantify the audiences of these new interactive electronic media. Although one could question the validity of today's media research techniques and findings for traditional media, we nevertheless have a history of this research and a relative comfort level with the findings. There is no audience research for the new media. Decisions to invest in one or another medium must, presently, be made almost solely on judgment.

26

Sampling Error

All media research is based on a sampling of the total population, a representative group whose media and product consumption patterns supposedly replicate those of the whole population, or those of a specified portion of the total population. Inherent in using a sample rather than the entire population is "sampling error"—the possible deviation of the reported finding from what might be the actual finding had the entire population been studied.

Making media decisions based on small differences among alternatives is therefore a shaky process. The planner must keep sampling error in mind whenever numerical comparisons among alternative media solutions are made because, in the real world, the exact opposite of what the research says *could* be true.

Table 26.1 shows the range in TV ratings that could be expected at each rating level in the typical Nielsen rating report. For example, if Program A has an average audience men rating of 10, the chances are about 95 out of 100 that the estimated rating would have differed by no more than 1.6 (+/− error) rating points from the rating had a complete census been undertaken. A 10 rated spot, therefore, could really deliver as low as an 8.4 rating or as high as an 11.6 rating. You will also note in the table that the "relative error" decreases as the absolute rating size increases, i.e., higher rated spots tend to be more "reliable." The relative error is derived by dividing the +/− error by the reported rating:

$$1.2 \div 5 = 24\%$$

Table 26.2 demonstrates the application of sampling error to a specific media decision of purchasing one or another TV program. Keep in mind that the same *directional* findings could be obtained for

Table 26.1. Sampling Error

Reported Rating	+/- Error*	Possible Rating	Relative Error
1	.6	.4–1.6	60 %
5	1.2	3.8–6.2	24
10	1.6	8.4–11.6	16
15	1.8	13.2–16.8	12
20	2.0	18.0–22.0	10

*At 95% confidence level.

Table 26.2. Application of Sampling Error in Purchase Decisions

	As Reported		Considering Sampling Error	
	Program A	Program B	Program A (–1.4 Rating)	Program B (+1.6 Rating)
Rating	10.0 (+/- 1.4)	8.0 (+/- 1.6)	8.4	9.4
Men	300,000	240,000	252,000	282,000
Cost/:30	$5,000	$5,000	$5,000	$5,000
CPP	$500	$625	$595	$532
CPM	$16.67	$20.83	$19.84	$17.73

any medium or media vehicle. Shown are two programs at varying rating/audience delivery but that cost the same amount of money for a 30-second ad. If the only evaluation device used to decide between the TV programs is cost-efficiency based on the reported audience delivery, then Program A should be chosen: a lower CPP and CPM.

However, if sampling error is considered, we see that Program A *could* produce an 8.4 rating and Program B *could* produce a 9.4 rating. If these possible variations are considered, then Program B *could* be more cost-efficient than Program A. The conclusion is that it is expeditious to purchase media simply on the basis of reported audiences, but it could also be the incorrect decision. Additionally, it should be clear at this point that numbers alone should never be used to make critical media decisions.

A sampling error exists in every research report that relies on a sampling of the population rather than on the entire population to gather its facts. By understanding this limitation, the planner or buyer can use research more as a guideline for decision making than as the final word.

27

How Much To Spend on Advertising

The amount of money that should be appropriated from the marketing budget to mount a successful advertising campaign is never clear-cut. With the exception of experimental formulas, there are no quick methods that we can use to define the optimum amount of money to be invested in advertising media. And even if there were magic answers, innumerable outside factors can influence the appropriation—from the profit margin of the brand, to the financial stability of the corporation, to competitive pressures, to the cost of media and advertising production.

The question of how much to spend requires detailed analysis to assess sales potential and affordability. The media planner's role in this decision-making process is limited. The planner can accumulate competitive advertising expenditures and guide the advertiser as to the cost of media and the audience delivery affordable at given budget levels.

How much to spend on advertising is a strategic decision. The advertising budget must be viewed as a function of the marketing and selling objectives of the brand or company. To have ambitious marketing goals supported by modest advertising budgets is irreconcilable. Conversely, it makes no financial sense to have an ambitious budget if the marketing goals are modest.

The role of advertising must be clearly defined, and its task must be decided before determining how much should be spent. Until the advertising task has been determined, you cannot apply the necessary discipline and available techniques to calculate how much money is required.

Factors to consider before choosing a spending technique include:

1. The market in which your brand (or service) will compete.

   The competitive environment must be selected to determine how much money you will need to accomplish your goals. For example, if you are advertising lemonade, you might decide to compete against all other lemonades, or all noncarbonated beverages, or all citrus beverages, or all refreshment beverages, including soft drinks. The amount of money being spent in each of these categories varies dramatically. Therefore, spending for your brand could represent a major or minor portion of the total category.

   Inherent in the competitive decision is the choice of demographic target. If you are going to compete only against other lemonades, for example, you might select an adult target, versus targeting adults, teens, and children if you choose to compete against all refreshment beverages. The more expansive the demographic target, the more money will be required to reach all consumer segments.

2. Where you will advertise.

   Invariably, all brands have pockets of strength and weakness across the country. Spending decisions must take these variations into consideration. The same rate of spending in every city or region will not necessarily produce the same results because of competitive environment variations from city to city and other environment and media cost factors.

   It is not sufficient simply to know the amount of sales in each city or region. You must determine the share of market in each location and the reason that share exists. For example, poor sales in a particular area could be the result of distribution deficiencies, pricing policies,, sales force weaknesses, or the strength of a specific local brand. Knowing the reasons will help you judge the contribution that might, or might not, be made by advertising. This, in turn, can guide you in spending policies.

3. The ability of advertising to effect a sales change or accomplish a specific goal.

   Depending on the objective to be achieved, the condition of the brand (or service) to be advertised, and the marketing environment as a whole, a decision could be made *not* to advertise. Advertising cannot be a panacea for all deficiencies. For example, if a product distribution deficiency exists whereby the product cannot reach the consumer, or is sold in inadequate quantities, any dollar spent in advertising would be wasted. If the product itself is inadequate and cannot match the competition, advertising might promote first-time trials among consumers but probably would not convince consumers to purchase the product again.

After these factors are considered, and a decision is made to advertise, a number of different techniques can be used to determine how much to spend and how to allocate those dollars. Four methods are discussed here.

Advertising/Sales Ratio Method

The advertising/sales ratio method is the most popularly used method for determining advertising budgets. Advertising expenditures are considered an integral part of the marketing budget of a product, and funds are set aside as a *cost of doing business.* The ratio used will vary widely among corporations (see Table 27.1), and often among different products within a corporation. For packaged goods, the advertis-

Table 27.1 Advertising as a Percent of Sales

Industry	A/S %*	Industry	A/S %*
Apparel	5.6	Household appliances	3.0
Auto supply stores	.9	Household A/V equipment	3.6
Beverages	7.5	Magazine publishing	5.6
Construction machinery	.2	Malt beverages	5.5
Department stores	2.6	Newspaper publishing	3.4
Elecronic computers	1.7	Perfume, cosmetics, toiletries	8.8
Food & like products	6.3	Radio broadcast stations	8.2
Games, toys	16.4	Soaps, detergents	9.9
Grocery stores	1.1	Sporting & athletic goods	6.4
Hotels, motels, tourist courts	3.6	TV broadcast stations	3.2

*Advertising/sales percentage.

Source: *Advertising Age.*

ing budget can also be expressed in terms of *case rate*—the amount of money to be spent for each case of product sold.

While the appropriation for advertising is part of the marketing budget, it is nevertheless the most vulnerable cost element. Manufacturing and distribution costs, as well as profit margins, are usually fixed. The only flexible marketing cost is the amount of money to be spent in advertising. Therefore, while budgets could be derived using the advertising/sales (A/S) ratio method, they are quite often subject to revision.

There are strengths and weaknesses in the A/S approach. The strengths are:

- It is self-correcting in regard to sales performance and maintains a consistent profit margin for the brand.

- It is relatively easy to manage the budget allocation.

- The relationship is easily understood and generally suits the interests of both the financial and marketing groups.

- An implicit incentive system operates whereby increased sales generate additional funds to support an aggressive advertising program, while the brand is penalized for poor sales.

The weaknesses of the A/S system are:

- The requirements for an advertising program do not always follow directly with sales, particularly when brand sales are declining and increased advertising may not be the cure.

- Considerable historical information is required to determine the correct A/S ratio.

- Variable A/S ratios should be used by area, which requires exhaustive analysis.

- The basic assumption of a direct linear relationship between advertising and sales might not be true.

Share of Advertising

In this system the advertising budget is chosen as a *share of total category advertising spending*. In the vernacular it is sometimes called the *share of noise,* where noise refers to the total advertising to which consumers are exposed.

As with the A/S method, there are strengths and weaknesses in this system. The strengths are:

- It positions your advertising budget competitively.

- You can react to competitive changes in advertising such as new brands entering the market.

- It places expectations for the advertising effort in a realistic perspective. For example, if you spend half as much as your nearest competitor, you cannot expect to exceed that competitor's share of market.

The weaknesses are:

- The information you gather might not be accurate because competitive advertising expenditure data is not easily obtained.

- The basic assumption of a direct relationship between share of advertising and share of market might not be true.

- Unless the right competitive market is defined, the wrong budget will be calculated.

- Share of advertising might be too narrow a view when one considers the influences of point-of-sale material, promotions, etc.

- Competitors could be dictating your budget and lead you into spending at the wrong rate.

Mathematical Models

A number of formulas have been developed to determine how much to spend. One formula, developed by the Hendry Corporation, for example, describes the interrelationships among advertising, share of market, and profits. From this, Hendry is able to determine how much money should be spent in advertising to maximize profits, and how much could be spent in advertising to maximize share of market.

The basic strength of using a mathematical model is that it usually includes all factors that influence customers' purchasing decisions—advertising, promotion, pricing, competitive environment, etc.

The weakness of using such a model is that you must spend time and money to find out if it works. It is impossible to determine if any model works without "real world" experience in the marketplace to determine if *X* budget produces *Y* result.

Task Method

The task method is where the media planner can play a significant part in the decision. This method requires the establishment of actionable marketing and media objectives and the writing of an advertising plan to achieve the task at hand.

As previously discussed, media objectives require extensive investigation and thought. However, after specific objectives are set forth, we can use simple mathematical procedures to determine the cost of purchasing media to accomplish these objectives. The objectives can be media-related (such as providing a certain level of reach and frequency during a given period of time); marketing related (such as the need to generate a certain amount of trial of a new product); or any combination of these.

The strength and weakness of this system are interrelated. If we know precisely what advertising levels are required to accomplish a task, the system is very powerful. However, if we do not know (and this is usually the case), this approach is highly subjective and therefore questionable.

Lastly, a task method approach does not concern itself with a brand's profitability. The amount of money required under this method may not bear any relation to what is affordable.

28

Media Objectives

All that we have discussed in previous chapters fuels the media plan by giving the media planner an understanding of how media forms work and how they can be analyzed. In this and the next chapter we will deal with media *objectives* and *strategies*—the essence of what a media plan is.

As a science, media planning requires the establishment of a hypothesis and a test of the variables that can prove or dismiss the hypothesis. The media plan, however, often does not evolve past the point of a theory. It can seldom be proven that a given plan is necessarily the best plan.

Much of media planning is judgment—informed judgment based on knowledge of the mechanics of each medium and some empirical evidence of how consumers react to media—but, nevertheless, judgment. Many of the decisions made on how to spend millions of advertising dollars are predicated more on convictions than provable facts. Many critical questions remain unanswered. Experience and good marketing/advertising judgment fill in the gaps.

We do not know, for example, how often a consumer must see an advertising message for Product X before the consumer buys Product X. And yet, the rate of exposure to advertising is one of the most important factors in devising a media plan. Exposure rate, or *frequency,* determines to a great extent which specific media are best, and how much money is necessary to do an effective job.

Despite a lack of crucial data, media decisions must be and are made. To guide the media planner in making correct decisions (more appropriately, practical and logical decisions that are agreed to by the advertiser), a structure is sought. We call this structure a media plan.

Basic Components of a Media Plan

Planning involves essentially three basic activities.

1. **Defining the marketing problem.** Do we know where our business is coming from and where the potential for increased business lies? Do we know the markets of greatest importance and greatest opportunity? Do we know who buys and who is most likely to buy? Do we need to stimulate trial or defend a franchise? Do we need to reach everybody or only a selective group of consumers? How often is the product used? How much product loyalty exists?

2. **Translating marketing requirements into actionable media objectives.** If the marketing objective is to stimulate trial among all potential consumers, then reaching many people is more important than reaching fewer people more frequently. If the product is purchased often, then reaching people more frequently might be a more appropriate tactic.

3. **Defining a media solution by formulating media strategies.** If reaching people is a primary objective, one should select affordable vehicles that will generate more reach than other media forms. If a specific demographic group is to be reached, media selection should be based on reaching that group effectively and efficiently.

Some might argue with the definitions of objectives and strategies and prefer to call strategies "tactics," etc. But these are arguments based on semantics. The intent of formulating objectives and strategies is to have a course of action with disciplined thinking, and if this is accomplished, any phraseology can be used.

The objectives of any media plan define *media goals*. The goals must be positive, action-oriented statements representing an extension of the marketing objectives and, therefore, also be marketing-goal oriented. The objectives cannot be innocuous. They must position the media plan relative to the market and the marketing plan. An objective that states:

Introduce Product X in order to achieve high levels of awareness.

does not provide direction. It says: Advertise. A more realistic and actionable objective guides the planner in assessing alternatives, such as:

Reach at least 80 percent of the potential market within the first month of advertising, ensuring that the average consumer will be exposed to a minimum of four advertising messages.

Or

Direct advertising to current and potential purchasers of Product Y by weighting current purchaser characteristics 60 percent and potential purchaser characteristics 40 percent.

Marketing Objectives

Because a media plan is an integral part of the marketing plan, the media objectives must reflect the marketing objectives. For example, we must ask if the product needs high levels of advertising that command consumers' attention (as with new products) or sustained advertising (as with established brands). Should advertising be scheduled in markets where the brand has its highest or lowest share? Are consumer promotions to be supported with advertising? Should media efforts be targeted to brand users, or nonusers?

Marketing Research

Marketing research can help define the market and the consumer. A number of research resources, such as Simmons, MRI, Scarborough, Media Audit, etc., are available to help with this investigation. Several life-style segmentation studies, such as Acorn, ClusterPLUS 2000, Micro Vision 50, and PRIZM, can be tied to this research to further define target audiences.

Creative Strategy

Creative strategy must be considered. If color is mandatory, the media planner would be hard pressed to rationalize the use of radio. The need for long copy versus short copy, or the knowledge that one advertisement will be created versus a pool of commercials, all have a bearing on media selection.

Promotion Strategy

The planner must be aware of the promotion strategy and, where appropriate, coordinate media activity with promotional programs. If consumer coupons are to be used, the planner must know timing and distribution requirements. How many coupons? How often? What kind of redemption is planned? What areas of the country? What target group of consumers?

Sales Data

Sales data are often a must. No brand has a flat sales picture in all of the United States. There are always areas of high and low development—areas where certain local factors or competitive forces play on the vitality of a brand. Sales data will also reveal seasonal sales patterns that may be important in scheduling advertising. The planner must also look at sales trends geographically. Seldom do the sales of a product increase or decrease in every market in the same way. Aberrations can usually be found and acted on.

Competitive Activity

Competitive activity must be fully understood. The planner must analyze competitive efforts and ascertain: Which media are being used? How often? In which areas of the United States? To what levels? Investigating competitive media investment could reveal opportunities for dominating media not used by competition, or suggest increased spending in media used extensively by competition.

Basic Questions

The best approach to formulating media objectives is to answer basic questions that encompass the general areas of audience, geography, scheduling requirements, copy needs, reach and frequency, and testing.

Audience

- Whom does the brand want to reach?

- What is the relative importance of each group?

A thorough objective recognizes the importance, or lack of importance, of each demographic cell. The planner should analyze audiences on the basis of age, sex, income, education, race, employment status, family size, marital status, possessions, life-style characteristics, and any other traits for which data are available. One must take care to ensure the creative strategy addresses the same people as defined in the media objectives.

There are usually one or two key demographic groups for most products or services, for example, women 18 to 34 years old. Too often, however, a planner analyzes this group alone, completely disregarding all other groups. By limiting analysis in this manner, he or she makes the conscious decision that groups not analyzed have zero value, and that media reaching these nondefined groups are providing unwanted delivery. The media planner should analyze all demographic characteristics, including race, to set values for each group and thereby determine a target audience that encompasses *all* people.

Market research generally reports on the value of each cell within a demographic category, such as women aged 18 to 34 within the category of age. But very little research is available to help in the decision of assigning values to each *category,* such as the value of age compared to that of income levels. If we do not place values on each category, then we have made the decision that each category is of equal importance. Logic dictates this is usually not the case.

An action-oriented objective providing clear direction to the planner might read:

Direct media to demographic groups in accordance with current consumption patterns:

	Percent of Total Consumption
Women 18–34	30
Women 35–49	20
Women 50+	10
Men 18–34	20
Men 35–49	15
Men 50+	5
Total	100 %

As stated earlier, demographic studies are important to the planning process, but are usually considered of secondary value to studies that define product *users.* Whenever user data is available to select media, it should be used.

Geography

- Where should the brand concentrate its advertising efforts?

- Are there markets that have minimal sales, and how should one value these markets?

- Are brand sales changing disproportionately in any markets?

- Is national advertising mandatory?

The planner should establish geographic targets for the smallest possible universe. In order of desirability, targets should be based on:

- Neighborhood

- County

- Market (metropolitan area, TV market, etc.)

- Sales area

- State

- Region

- County size

The planner should recognize the sales or sales potential in each geographic area, as well as any other ingredient deemed important, such as income, housing, mobility, etc. Often, we can use related data as a predictor of product sales: Automobile mileage can be used to predict tire sales; temperature can be used to forecast sales of hot weather soft drinks.

It would be beneficial to establish a target for each geographic denominator and then allocate media delivery to each in accordance with these targets. Quite often it is necessary to do extensive sales analyses to establish targets by market.

After all pertinent information is amassed, we need to decide which of two philosophies will be used to allocate advertising. There are two basic philosophies:

1. **Advertise where the business is.** This is basically a defensive posture. It protects the existing franchise and simultaneously seeks to develop more business on the assumption that increases in brand sales can be achieved most efficiently where the brand is currently strong. It is easier to build on an existing base where product distribution has been established and where there is apparent consumer awareness and acceptance of your product. Current nonusers in these areas have a greater propensity to become users than nonusers in areas where your product sales are low.

2. **Advertise where the business is not.** This philosophy is offensive. It is based on the belief that changing consumer demands, as well as changes in product formulation for your brand

or the competitive brands, result in brand switching. Advertising in these areas would therefore announce your presence and keep your brand on consumers' minds should they decide to switch brands. To implement this philosophy successfully, you must first ensure other marketing factors: You must have the right product for the consumers, competitive pricing, widespread distribution, sufficient inventory position to restock for repurchase after initial trial, and good display. Advertising alone will not produce sales, nor remedy marketing deficiencies.

One can use either philosophy, or some combination of both, depending on the marketing strategy. In any case, the objective at this stage of the analysis is to assign a "target percentage" to each U.S. market. The target represents the *share* that market should receive of the total advertising effort. The target percentage for all markets combined must equal 100 percent.

Scheduling

- To what degree should the brand recognize seasonal sales patterns?

- Are there any discernible patterns?

- How important is the introductory versus the sustaining period?

- Should competitive advertising efforts be countered?

The planner must formulate precise direction for each of these areas. Whenever possible, you should use the most specific calendar units (days, weeks, months). The extent of any effort must be quantified in order to show emphasis clearly. For example, clear direction is shown in the following kinds of objectives:

- Spend advertising dollars in accordance with the percentage of sales each month.

- Allocate no more than 60 percent of advertising expenditures during the introductory 13-week period.

- Increase advertising activity by 50 percent during each of the three planned promotion periods. Precede the promotion by one week and run concurrently during the remaining four weeks of the promotion.

- Concentrate all advertising from Wednesday to Saturday in order to reach potential Product X buyers immediately prior to the highest usage day, Sunday.

Copy

- What are the basic requirements for color, audio, visual?

- How does the complexity of the message affect copy length?

- What is the brand's creative experience?

Copy is obviously of extreme importance to any viable advertising effort. Regardless of the impact of the media plan, if it does not properly reflect the copy strategy, the entire campaign suffers. The media planner should not, however, be the mistress of the copywriter. It is important for both to work together to create the best copy in the best medium, and this should happen in the early stages of planning. The copywriter should be made aware of the media ramifications of certain decisions as should the media planner have a complete understanding of the copy needs.

Coupons

- Will the media plan require a consumer promotion in the form of a media-distributed coupon?

- How many coupons will be distributed?

- How much reach will be required?

A number of advertising plans contain a promotional effort that can be either trade-oriented or consumer-oriented. Trade promotions could take many forms, such as in-store displays, cost allowances (discounts) for purchasing certain quantities of product or purchasing at certain times of the year, sales contests, etc. These kinds of trade promotions do not generally require a consumer media effort.

A promotion directed to the consumer does require media support. Although the label of this effort is promotion, as opposed to advertising, the two must work in concert. If the marketing objective requires distribution of a cents-off coupon in order to counter competitive efforts or promote consumer trial, then this must be translated into an actionable media objective so the media planner can schedule appropriate media to deliver these coupons into the consumers' hands.

Reach and Frequency

- What reach level is needed?

- How much frequency is required?

- Should reach/frequency levels vary by market?

- Should reach/frequency levels vary by time of the year?

The number of people you need to reach with advertising and how often you need to reach them has the most demonstrable effect on a media plan. If it is possible to have a precise objective that clearly establishes how many people need to be reached and how often, this will significantly influence your choices of which media forms to consider, how much of each medium can be used, the number of weeks that advertising is affordable, or the budget that is necessary to achieve this objective.

Unfortunately, this objective is sometimes written after a plan is constructed and the delivery of that plan is determined. While this guarantees the objective will be achieved and will thereby make the media planner a genius at the task, it is a pointless exercise. If a predetermined level of advertising intensity is desirable or needed based on past performance, competitive pressure, or judgment, then the planner should state that level in the objectives—prior to devising the actual media plan.

Testing

- Should a media or copy test be conducted?

- What information can be garnered with a test?

Testing should always be considered in every media plan. There are too many unanswered questions to avoid testing. When one considers that an average media or copy test represents a negligible part of most large advertising budgets, the obvious conclusion is that testing should be continuous. Regardless of the media plan recommended, there is always room to conduct a test. For example:

- An unused medium—magazines if you are using TV, or radio if you are using magazines.

- Any *new* medium, such as the interactive media forms now in development.

- Media mix—magazines and TV versus either alone, or radio plus newspapers.

- Copy length—ten-second commercials if the plan calls for 30 seconds, or half pages instead of full pages.

- Scheduling—flighting advertising with hiatus periods as opposed to continuous advertising, or concentrating in one television daypart rather than dispersing announcements through two or more dayparts.

Representative areas of the United States should be carved out in which to conduct testing. The areas should not only be a microcosm of total U.S. demography, but should also be representative of average product consumption, as well as having appropriate media availability in which to conduct the test.

You should give the test a fair chance to work. There is no magic timetable for a test after which period you can draw valid conclusions. But it is fair to assume that a media or copy test conducted in the marketplace will take weeks, or months, or perhaps a year before its thrust is felt at the consumer level.

Finally, don't have a knee-jerk reaction to whatever is in vogue or what you might think is a testable proposition. All tests cost time and money. If it is a new or untried traditional medium, creative people must spend time and money developing creative for the medium. The media planner/buyer must spend time and money (salary) to develop the plan and buy the media. The advertiser must spend time and money to pay for the media being tested. Topical investigation and reporting is a prudent first step. If there is a consensus to proceed, then a full-blown test plan should be written.

In some cases, not all objectives can be realistically met. For example, there may be an objective to reach at least 80 percent of a target group, and a second objective that requires advertising continuously throughout the sales season. Media availability and cost could prohibit the planner from accomplishing both of these objectives. It is therefore wise to prioritize the objectives in order to have a clear direction in the decision-making process. If reach is given a greater priority than continuity of advertising, then the planner, when faced with the above situation, can elect to provide the needed levels of reach for as long a period as is affordable without necessarily advertising throughout the sales season.

Summary

Media objectives define media goals and should be action oriented.

The best way to define objectives is to answer questions that have a bearing on media selection and usage.

Objectives should be established before the media plan is written, even if the plan recommended does not meet every objective precisely.

Testing on a continuous basis can lead to answering critical questions pertinent to the brand.

29

Media Strategies

Media strategies are the solutions to the media objectives. Strategy statements reflect the specific course of action to be taken with media:

- Which media will be used?
- How often will each be used?
- How much of each medium will be used?
- During which periods of the year?

Devising media strategy requires that the planner have an in-depth knowledge of media characteristics—how they work, how they are consumed, and how they can be used to generate a desired effect. The planner must also have an understanding of the media marketplace—what the availability and cost structure of each medium is at a given point in time. If the planner decides primetime network television should be scheduled for April to achieve a particular objective, he or she must know if the television networks have unsold inventory for this month and, if so, what the cost of these commercial units might be.

A number of media alternatives are available to achieve media objectives. The planner's job is to find the best medium, or combination of media, that will produce the best overall effect relative to the needs of the advertised brand. This requires extensive analysis.

The following are examples of how the planner might approach media analysis in order to accomplish several specific objectives. In all cases, the examples are illustrative of a particular situation and should not be construed as the only way to approach media analysis. Additionally, all examples restrict consideration to one or two audience segments and a few media alternatives. Actual analysis of media alternatives requires far more extensive tabulating than presented in these examples.

Target Audience Objective

Let us assume we have established an objective to recognize the relative importance of men and women in the purchase decision of Product X:

Select media on the basis of a 40%/60% weighting for men and women respectively.

For illustration ease, let us also assume that the creative units available for this advertising effort are 30-second television commercials, 60-second radio commercials, and full-page four-color magazine advertisements.

The first step in investigating which media might best suit the objective is to analyze the audience composition of the various media in order to establish a general idea of how each medium distributes its audience. Table 29.1 shows, for example, that the average primetime network adult audience is composed of 44 percent men and 56 percent women.

This overview would indicate that the exclusive use of daytime television would probably not achieve the objective because only a

Table 29.1. Audience Composition

	Unit	Men	Women	Total
Television	:30			
Daytime		21	79	100%
Prime		44	56	100%
Cable (prime)		52	48	100%
Network radio	:30	50	50	100%
Newspaper	1/2 Page B/W	47	53	100%
Magazines	1P4C			
General		44	56	100%
Men's		82	18	100%
Women's		13	87	100%
Outdoor #50	Posters	55	45	100%

small portion of its adult audience is composed of men. Likewise, the exclusive use of men's magazines would be deficient in delivering women.

We should analyze audience composition for the specific media vehicles within broad categories. Audience composition varies widely among vehicles within a general category. The analysis, therefore, should include television program types, radio program types, and specific magazines, so the planner can seek out opportunities that might be masked by generalities.

The second step is to analyze the various media on the basis of actual delivery and cost-efficiency. The higher the affordable level of delivery, the lower the cost-per-thousand. Higher absolute delivery will also result in increased reach and/or frequency.

Table 29.2 shows the gross impressions for each media form for men, women, and total adults.

In order to accomplish the objective, however, the audience delivery must be weighted as stated: 40 percent men/60 percent women. By multiplying the men impressions of each medium by 40 percent and the women impressions by 60 percent, and then adding the products, "weighted" impressions can be established (see Table 29.3). Inasmuch as the impressions are devalued for each audience segment, the weighted impressions are not "real" numbers, but merely an indication of the *relative* delivery of each medium.

Table 29.2. Gross Impressions Affordable within $1 Million Budget

		Millions of People			
	Unit	**Men**	**Women**	**Total**	**CPM**
Television	:30				
Daytime		65	250	315	$3.17
Prime		60	75	135	7.41
Cable (prime)		70	65	135	7.41
Network radio	:30	250	250	500	2.00
Newspaper	1/2 Page B/W	40	45	85	11.76
Magazines	1P4C				
General		140	185	325	3.08
Men's		135	30	165	6.06
Women's		20	140	160	6.25
Outdoor #50	Posters	385	315	700	1.43

Table 29.3. Weighted Delivery: 40 Percent Men/60 Percent Women

	Unit	Unweighted	Weighted	CPM
		Millions of People		
Television	:30			
Daytime		315	176	$5.68
Prime		135	69	14.49
Cable (prime)		135	67	14.93
Network radio	:30	500	250	4.00
Newspaper	1/2 Page B/W	85	43	23.26
Magazines	1P4C			
General		325	167	5.99
Men's		165	72	13.89
Women's		160	92	10.85
Outdoor #50	Posters	700	343	2.92

Having established weighted impression delivery, the cost-per-thousand can be calculated for each media form (see Table 29.3).

Based on cost-per-thousand, the media planner would assign priorities to the media shown in this table as follows: Most cost-efficient, outdoor; next, network radio; next daytime TV, and so forth.

Not all media have the same "communication value." Television, for example, is an intrusive medium—commercials are broadcast into a person's home without invitation. Some argue that this intrusive quality is advantageous because the consumer does not have to seek out the advertising. Others might argue that magazines offer advertisers the opportunity for full copy exposition in high-fidelity color that the reader can refer to again and again.

Whether based on research data or judgment which considers the copy execution or competitive position of the brand, the planner should assign a weight to each medium that represents the medium's relative ability to communicate the message effectively. If medium X is considered to be only one-half as effective as medium Y, then medium X should be given a weight of 50, and medium Y a weight of 100.

Table 29.4 further weights the impressions shown in this exercise, using hypothetical values for each media form. For example, 176 million impressions for daytime network TV times a value of 75 percent equals *valued* impressions of 132 million.

Table 29.4. Valued Impressions

	Millions of People			
	Value	**Weighted**	**Valued**	**CPM**
Television				
Daytime	75	176	132	$7.58
Prime	100	69	69	14.49
Cable (prime)	65	67	44	22.73
Network radio	50	250	125	8.00
Newspaper	80	43	34	29.41
Magazines				
General	90	167	150	6.67
Men's	90	72	65	15.38
Women's	90	92	83	12.05
Outdoor #50	25	343	86	11.63

Table 29.5. Media Ranking by CPM

	Unit	**Unweighted**	**Weighted**	**Valued**
Television	:30			
Daytime		4	3	2
Prime		7	7	6
Cable (prime)		7	8	8
Network radio	:30	2	2	3
Newspaper	1/2 Page B/W	9	9	9
Magazines	1P4C			
General		3	4	1
Men's		5	6	7
Women's		6	5	5
Outdoor #50	Posters	1	1	4

At this point, the planner has evaluated all media on the basis of their ability to deliver a weighted target audience of 40 percent men/ 60 percent women, and has further weighted each medium on the basis of communication values. Based on a cost-per-thousand ranking (with the lowest CPM being the first choice), the planner would have assigned the priorities to each media form shown in Table 29.5.

If cost-per-thousand were the sole criterion in selecting media, the first dollar spent should be allocated to general magazines. General magazines should be used to the level deemed appropriate before daytime television is added to the media schedule, and so forth down the line until the budget is exhausted.

Cost-per-thousand alone, however, should never be the sole criterion in selecting media. Before being able to make an intelligent media choice, one must consider many other factors, such as reach, frequency of exposure, reach accumulation over time, competitive efforts, promotional needs, etc. No media plan should have but one objective that requires only the achievement of delivering gross impressions at the lowest cost-per-thousand.

Nevertheless the above is useful as one ingredient in an analysis of media alternatives. When additional analyses are made that address the other objectives of the media plan, the planner can then evaluate the various media options in terms of achieving all objectives combined with the best alternative.

Geographic Objective

Another objective in a media plan might be to allocate advertising dollars to each U.S. market in proportion to sales.

There are usually pronounced differences market to market in a brand's sales, competitive pressures, distribution penetration, and a host of other marketing variables. It's beneficial to use these pieces of data to allocate advertising to each market relative to local market phenomena.

The planner must first make a complete geographic business analysis that includes all pertinent marketing information. At minimum, this analysis should include product sales, but it usually includes other factors affecting sales and sales potential.

The assumption at this point is that the general media forms being used in the plan have already been selected: Television, magazines, newspapers, radio, outdoor, etc. The decision to be made is how much *national* media (e.g., network TV) and how much *local* (e.g., Spot TV) should be used. The objective is to fit the delivery of the media to the local market targets.

The easiest way to match advertising delivery to preestablished goals in each market is to use only local media forms: Spot TV, spot radio, newspapers, outdoor, etc. The use of national media (e.g., network TV) would result in a mismatch in a number of markets. National media deliver their messages at different levels throughout the

United States and almost never in proportion to the targets established for your brand.

As shown in Exhibit 29.1, ten primetime TV announcements will deliver 70 men TRPs in the *average* market. TRP delivery will vary from market to market because of differences in viewing patterns—in this example, delivery ranges from a high of 80 TRPs to a low of 49 TRPs.

Looking at national magazine circulation, we again see wide variations from one geographic area to another. As shown in Table 29.6,

Exhibit 29.1. Average Men TRPs by TV Market.
Top 25 Markets—10 Primetime TV Programs

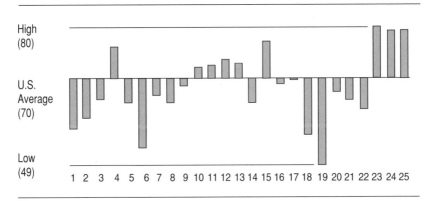

Table 29.6. Magazine Circulation by Geographic Area

| Area | % Population | Index (% Circulation/% Population) | | |
		Time	Reader's Digest	National Geographic
New England	5.1	149	102	129
Mid-Atlantic	14.7	124	90	88
E. No. Central	16.6	95	104	95
W. No. Central	7.0	96	130	107
South Atlantic	17.8	94	97	93
E. So. Central	6.1	64	92	67
W. So. Central	10.8	72	98	81
Mountain	5.7	95	125	136
Pacific	16.2	109	91	122
Total	100.0	100	100	100

for example, *Time* has an index of 149, indicating that 7.6 percent of its circulation is in the New England region, compared to a population count of 5.1 percent. If you wished to deliver circulation in direct proportion to population, *Time* (as well as other magazines) would not achieve your goal. Some areas would receive proportionately more circulation than you wished, while others would receive less.

National media can be used, however, without overdelivering any market if the extent of their use is limited. The trick is to combine the proper levels of both national and local media to obtain optimum results in both local markets and for the United States as a whole.

Either of two methods can be used to allocate national and local media to local markets:

1. **Dollar Allocation.** This method apportions the total dollar spending of all media combined to each market relative to the target percentage. If Chicago is targeted to receive 6 percent of the total U.S. investment, then 6 percent of your total media budget should be spent in Chicago.

2. **Impression allocation.** This method allocates the total impression delivery of all media combined to each market, again relative to the target percentage. If Chicago is targeted at 6 percent, it should receive 6 percent of the media plan's total impression delivery.

The methods are based on two distinct strategies and produce significantly different results.

The dollar allocation system:

- Matches sales dollars with advertising dollars.

- Equalizes return on investment in each market.

- Limits spending in inefficient markets, thus producing more impression delivery overall.

- Presupposes that dollars should be controlled without specific regard to the levels of advertising delivery in each market.

The impression allocation system:

- Produces an unequalized dollar investment in each market.

- Does not relate advertising dollars to sales dollars.

- Produces fewer impressions overall.

- Produces impressions (or GRPs) in each market in proportion to the market's target.

- Presupposes that consumers react to advertising delivery, not dollars per se.

When purchasing national media, we assume that the investment in each market is in direct proportion to the delivery in that market. All markets therefore have the same cost-per-thousand. A package of 10 primetime network TV announcements cost approximately $1,000,000 and will deliver 70 men TRPs on a national basis, equal to 60 million men impressions. The men cost-per-thousand of this package is $16.67. We have already established that TRP delivery varies from market to market. Therefore, to establish the number of impressions in each market, we need to multiply the local market TRP delivery by the TV base in that market. By then multiplying the local market impressions by the *national* CPM, we establish the prorated cost for a national plan in each market. In Table 29.7 we see that New York, with 4,637,000 men impressions, accounts for $77,300 of the $1 million plan.

The same dynamics apply to the allocation of network radio dollars to each local market: Apportion total U.S. expenditures proportionately to each local market on the basis of local market impression delivery. In print media, the average national cost-per-thousand is applied to each market based on local circulation.

After local market spending is established for national media forms, various combinations of national and local media can be analyzed to determine the optimum combination: That combination that will meet

Table 29.7. Allocating Network TV Spending to Local Markets

	Men Impressions (in 1,000s)	CPM	Total Cost
New York	4,637	$16.67	$77,300
Los Angeles	3,227	16.67	53,800
Chicago	2,148	16.67	35,800
Philadelphia	1,758	16.67	29,300
San Francisco	1,446	16.67	24,100
Remaining Markets	46,784	16.67	779,700
Total U.S.	60,000	$16.67	$1,000,000

Table 29.8. Dollar Allocation

Plan I—Only Network TV

	% U.S. Sales	Impressions (in $1,000s)	CPM	Expenditures	% Total
A	50	28,000	$5.00	$140,000	40
B	30	28,000	5.00	140,000	40
C	20	14,000	5.00	70,000	20
Total	100	70,000	$5.00	$350,000	100

Plan II—Network TV & Spot TV

	% U.S. Sales	Target Budget	Network	Spot	Total	% Total
A	50	$175,000	$70,000	$105,000	$175,000	50
B	30	105,000	70,000	35,000	105,000	30
C	20	70,000	35,000	35,000	70,000	20
Total	100	$350,000	$175,000	$175,000	$350,000	100

local market *targets* and deliver meaningful levels of advertising in each medium being used.

Table 29.8 shows two different media plans: Plan I is composed of only network TV; Plan II is a combination of network and Spot TV. Both have the same $350,000 budget to be spent in three markets combined. For simplicity, let us assume that the United States is composed of only three markets. The strategy in the media plan dictates that advertising expenditures should be in direct proportion to sales in each market. Market A, therefore, should receive 50 percent of all dollars because it accounts for 50 percent of sales. Using the dollar allocation system, we determine that Plan I spends 40 percent of the total budget in Market A—underdelivering the 50 percent goal. Market B is overspent. Plan II, however, limits the spending in network TV to allocate the remaining funds to Spot TV in the proportions needed to produce the proper overall spending pattern. As shown, Plan II expenditures by market are in direct proportion to sales.

There are situations where underspending in a local market would be tolerated: In those instances where certain markets, regardless of their sales potential, are excluded from advertising consideration for any number of reasons or where the level of national advertising to be purchased is below minimum acceptable criteria. Overspending in a local market can also be tolerated under certain situations (e.g., when prior commitments to national media force the investment).

The procedures used for an impression allocation are similar to those of the dollar allocation. The planner calculates impressions for the total of all media being used and apportions them to each market based on local viewing/reading habits. The national delivery is subtracted from the target delivery to yield the number of impressions one needs to purchase via local media in order to meet the target. Local media impressions delivery is priced to determine affordability within the total media budget. Nearly always, the total target impression delivery costs more than the budget allows. You therefore need to make a prorated adjustment in each market to bring the total advertising plan within budget.

Scheduling Objective

Every media plan should have a scheduling objective to guide the planner in allocating media across the year. *When* advertising is delivered is often a critical issue. Advertising for suntan lotion should obviously be concentrated in those months when people need suntan lotion. Advertising for a product consumed to varying degrees throughout the year, however, presents a less obvious scheduling requirement. As stated earlier, you must make a complete investigation of the brand's needs vis-à-vis its competitive position and historical sales trend. These marketing considerations can be translated into actionable media objectives that will address, in broad strokes, the general requirement for the timing of advertising across the year.

Beyond the general timing consideration, the media planner should also consider the strategy of *flighting* versus *continuous* advertising. Some definitions:

- **Flighting** refers to periodic waves of advertising interspersed with periods of total inactivity.

- **Continuous** advertising is a schedule with little or no variations in pressure.

- **Pulsing** is a combination of the above two concepts: A continuous base of support augmented by intermittent bursts of heavy pressure.

Exhibit 29.2 demonstrates the three techniques by showing the number of weekly TRPs that can be scheduled using each pattern. All

Exhibit 29.2. Scheduling Techniques

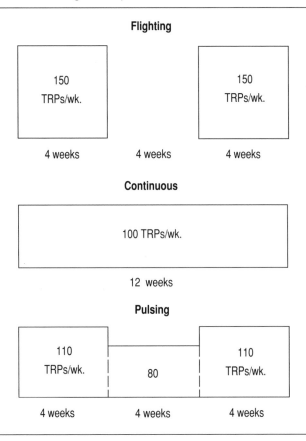

three techniques encompass a total of 1,200 TRPs over a 12-week period.

Audience accumulation of flighted and continuous schedules at equal rating levels is identical over the *long run*. All three schedules will accumulate the same number of Target Rating Points (assuming equal costs during the entire advertising campaign period); all three schedules will reach the same number of people with equivalent frequency; all three schedules will distribute impressions among the different audience segments in about the same manner.

Audience accumulation of flighted and continuous schedules, however, will vary considerably over the *short run*. As the frequency distribution shown in Table 29.9 (based on the flighted and continuous schedules shown in Exhibit 29.2) points out, the flighted schedule produces slightly higher total reach (1 + frequency) over a four-week period than the continuous schedule, but substantially more reach at

Table 29.9. Frequency Distribution (Four-Week Schedule)

Number of Exposures	Percent Reach		Reach Difference
	Continuous Schedule	Flighted Schedule	
1 or more	91	95	4
2 or more	78	86	8
3 or more	64	76	12
4 or more	50	66	16
5 or more	38	56	18
6 or more	28	47	19
7 or more	20	39	19
8 or more	14	31	17
9 or more	10	25	15
10 or more	6	20	14
Schedule:	100 TRPs/week	150 TRPs/week	

the higher frequency levels. If the media planner establishes an "effective reach" level of at least four exposures, for example, then the flighted schedule has a distinct advantage in the short run.

Although much research has been conducted to answer the question of how much frequency is required to communicate the advertising message effectively, no one study has provided a definitive answer. The hypotheses of all these studies are:

- There is a direct relationship between frequency of exposure during a given period of time and advertising effectiveness.

- There is a minimum rate of exposure (frequency) below which the sales motivation value is either unproductive or marginal.

- There is a ceiling of frequency above which additional exposure is either unproductive or produces diminishing returns.

- There is decay in recall levels and established attitudes during hiatuses.

- Advertising effectiveness does *not* immediately cease when advertising is discontinued.

The dimensions of these factors may vary in accordance with the product's purchase cycle, stage of product development, product category, competitive environment, creative execution, media selection, and media weights. If the media planner believes the hypotheses to be correct, and gives consideration to all these factors, then he or she establishes an effective frequency level against which to analyze both flighted and continuous scheduling patterns.

A number of alternative methods for scheduling media can produce the effect of both flighting and continuous advertising simultaneously. For example, if the media plan is composed of two television dayparts, or national and local media, or two different media forms, each of the components can be flighted in an alternating pattern. Additionally, different broadcast stations, or different magazines, can be scheduled at different times producing a flighted effect for specific vehicles, and a continuous effect across the media form (see Exhibit 29.3).

The media planner should bear in mind that even continuous advertising is received by the consumer in a flighted pattern. A schedule of one announcement per week in network television, for example, will be seen by some people only once, some people only twice, etc. The period between exposures to your advertising is indeed a hiatus in the consumer's perception. The technique of flighting advertising produces higher levels of activity during certain periods of time. This higher level of activity, in turn, generates higher levels of frequency of exposure and thereby shortens the hiatus period between exposures.

Exhibit 29.3. Flighting Patterns

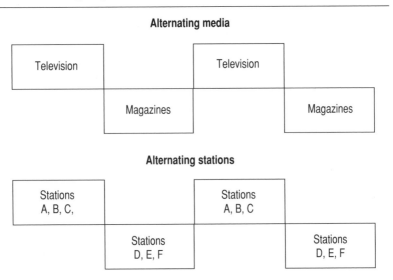

Coupon Objective

The media plan might require coupons be distributed via consumer media. The extent of distribution (number of coupons and geography) is outlined in the objective.

It is now the media planner's role to select the specific media to carry the coupons.

In addition to typical media considerations, factors of primary importance in evaluating media vehicles for coupon promotions include:

- The coupon form to be used and the availability of that form in media.

- Circulation distribution requirements—how many coupons are to be distributed.

- The distribution method of the media vehicle.

- Advertising space and redemption costs.

- Duplication among media vehicles.

There are several coupon forms, and several media types carry coupons. An insert coupon can be carried in magazines as a pop-up card, usually requiring the purchase of a back-up page on which the card will lie. Inserts can also be distributed via direct mail, either as a co-op effort with other advertisers or as a solo venture. Most advertisers do not do solo couponing via direct mail because list generation and mailing costs are too high. Sharing these basic costs in a co-op mailing reduces the distribution cost substantially with only a slight reduction in redemption rate.

Many newspapers and supplements also make available free-standing inserts—preprinted material not physically attached to the publication, but carried within the pages, or between sections. On-page coupons can be purchased in magazines, newspapers, or supplements, without any cost premium over the usual rate for space. Stick-on coupons can be purchased in supplements. The edge of the card coupon is glued to the page.

Coupon redemption rates vary by type of coupon and by medium. Table 29.10 shows the average redemption rates for a wide variety of coupon types as tabulated by A. C. Nielsen.

If there is a marketing objective for total redemption, the media planner can estimate the number of coupons that will be redeemed by using the following redemption rates for each medium considered. This redemption data can also be used in combination with the media

Table 29.10. Coupon Redemption Rates

Newspaper on-page	2.8 %
Newspaper co-op	3.0
Magazine on-page	2.4
Magazine pop-up	5.1
Sunday Supplement—free-standing insert	4.3
Sunday Supplement—on-page	2.4
Direct mail	8.0

selection data (discussed later) to determine the cost-per-thousand of coupons redeemed by medium.

Magaziners will generally limit the number of coupons accepted to one per signature (consists of 16 to 24 folded pages bound together to form a section). Some publications restrict the face value of a single coupon to the cost of their cover price, while some place a limit on the total cumulative value of insert coupons within a single issue. Both these restrictions are an attempt to reduce misredemption. When a magazine insert coupon that is redeemable at the store is involved, circulation is generally limited to subscription copies, to deter possible misredemption at the newsstand or distribution level.

For promotional use, media *circulation* values often override total audience measurements because passalong audiences may not have an equal opportunity to receive the offer because of its previous extraction by the primary reader. Additionally, one should give consideration to the value of an advertising page to the secondary reader if that page has been mutilated because the primary reader has cut out the coupon.

Therefore, media *coverage* should be analyzed on the basis of the number of copies distributed, rather than total audience only. Of primary importance is duplication among media vehicles. That combination of vehicles with the *least* duplication is most desirable as it will extend reach of the program to as many different prospects as possible and limit the delivery of more than one coupon to the same person.

The total cost of a coupon promotion is composed of the cost of advertising space and the absolute coupon redemption. Thus the type of coupon selected and the rate of redemption that can be expected from each media vehicle are important considerations when evaluating media alternatives.

Reach/Frequency Objective

Assume an objective has been established to maximize reach of women 18 to 49 with a minimum of four advertising exposures per month (once per week). For demonstration ease, let us assume that network television has been chosen as the only medium to be used. The planner is now faced with deciding among network TV dayparts, and if a combination of dayparts are to be used, what proportions of each should be used.

The planner could start the analysis by devising as many alternative schedules as are affordable within the given budget. Shown in Table 29.11 are seven alternatives (though the number of alternatives is nearly infinite).

The seven levels are different in many ways (see Table 29.12). They produce different numbers of announcements, different TRP lev-

Table 29.11. Alternative Media Plan Considerations

	Women 18–49 TRPs				
Plan	Daytime	Prime	Early News	Late Evening	Total
A	280	—	—	—	280
B	—	90	—	—	90
C	—	—	100	—	100
D	—	—	—	120	120
E	140	45	—	—	185
F	—	45	50	—	95
G	—	45	—	60	105

Table 29.12. Media Plan Comparisons

Plan	TRPs	CPM*	Number of Spots	Reach	Frequency
A	280	$3.75	80	43	6.5
B	90	11.75	13	47	1.9
C	100	10.50	29	40	2.5
D	120	8.75	44	43	2.8
E	185	5.75	47	39	4.7
F	95	11.00	21	42	2.3
G	105	10.00	29	38	2.8

*Rounded.

els, different cost-efficiencies, and different total reach and average frequency. The only thing in common among the plans is that they are all national in scope (network television), and each costs the same amount of money ($1 million).

None of this information, however, is useful in making a decision if the objective is *effective* reach (maximize reach of women with a minimum of four advertising exposures per month). The number of announcements is a function of the budget and the cost per commercial unit—it does not reveal anything about reach. Total women 18 to 49 TRPs is informational and offers an indication of the gross delivery, but also does not reveal facts about reach. Cost-per-thousand is useful for assessing the efficiency of one alternative versus another, but again, no information about reach. Total women 18 to 49 reach/frequency, at first blush, might be used as the criterion for selecting one plan over another, but *average* frequency does not indicate the percentage of women who will be exposed to at least four advertising messages.

The planner must take the analysis a step further by calculating a frequency distribution for each plan. Table 29.13, based on a frequency distribution of each plan, exhibits the percentage of women 18 to 49 who will be exposed to at least four advertising messages.

Based on Table 29.13, the planner would opt for Plan A, composed of all daytime TV. This plan reaches more women who will be exposed to at least four advertising messages. If the planner had not done a frequency distribution, he or she might have chosen Plan B because it generates more total reach than the other plans.

Although this analysis seems very straightforward, seldom does the planner have the flexibility to select media vehicles on the basis of accomplishing only one objective. Additionally, all analyses are com-

Table 29.13. Effective Reach Comparisons

Plan	Women 18–49 Reach at 4.0 + Frequency Level
A	28
B	3
C	15
D	23
E	18
F	13
G	10

Table 29.14. Weighting Media by Communications Values

	Women GRPs	×	Value	=	Weighted Women GRPs
Primetime	45		100%		45
Daytime	140		75%		105
Total	185				150

plicated by a number of other factors that have an effect on how the planner addresses each medium at any point in time.

Costs, for example, fluctuate among network TV dayparts throughout the year based on supply and demand. Hypothetically, primetime network might be less cost-efficient than late night network in one calendar quarter, and more cost-efficient in another. The lower the cost-per-thousand, the more TRPs that can be purchased within a set budget. The more TRPs that can be purchased, the higher the reach and/or frequency that can be produced.

Let us take the above exercise one step further and assume that "communication values" are part of the media analysis. If we assume, for example, that daytime's communication value is 75 percent that of primetime, we could make a totally different strategy decision based on an analysis of effective reach. If primetime TRPs are valued at 100 percent, and daytime TRPs at 75 percent, then the weighted TRPs for Plan E are 150 (as opposed to 185 when each daypart is given full value) as shown in Table 29.14.

If the planner calculates a frequency distribution based on the above weighted TRPs, the reach of women 18 to 49 at the 4+ frequency level is 15. This is the same effective reach as generated by Plan C (all early evening news). If an evaluation of effective reach does not reveal major differences among plan alternatives, or if other objectives bear importantly on media usage, then the planner must use other criteria to decide which media are most appropriate for accomplishing the objectives of the plan.

Testing Objective

Every media plan should have an objective to test advertising. Media/marketing tests are conducted to gain knowledge so better decisions can be made in the future. All tests have two things in common:

- They minimize the risk of incorrectly spending media funds.

- They are learning experiences from which we can extrapolate results for further use.

The most common test is of a complete marketing/media program developed for a new product prior to its national launch. Additionally, there are a number of other tests that can be conducted, all of which can provide useful information:

- **Spending levels.** A test of increased or decreased spending compared to the current level.

- **Allocation philosophy.** Spending where the business is versus where the business is not.

- **Scheduling.** Testing the effects of continuous advertising versus flighting.

- **Media mix.** Using different media than currently used, either exclusively or in combination with current media.

- **Copy length.** Using 30-second versus 60-second commercials, or full pages versus half pages, etc.

Regardless of the test conducted, it is important to construct the test plan for the geographic area in which the plan would be implemented if the test is successful. For a new product planned for a national launch, the test must be national in scope. For a regionally distributed product (e.g., beer marketed only east of the Mississippi), the test plan must include all states in that region.

It is important that the national plan be translated down to the test market(s) rather than vice versa. In this manner, one is able to construct a plan that has national implication. If a plan is devised for the test market only, it might not be projectable to the universe, nor be affordable or implementable on a national basis.

Test markets should be representative of the universe to which results will be projected. If a national media plan is tested in markets that do not represent the United States in terms of sales, competitive activity, socioeconomic factors, media consumption patterns, etc., results from the test might not be representative of what could happen in the United States as a whole.

Control markets should also be selected to read the effects of the current plan compared to the effects in the test markets where the media usage has been altered. Control markets should be selected on the same basis as test markets and therefore be carefully matched to the test markets. Both control and test markets should have adequate auditing facilities and/or sales data in order to make proper comparisons.

The national plan should be constructed for the period in which it will run (assuming the test results are positive) rather than for the period in which it will be tested. If a national plan is constructed for calendar year 1997, and tested in 1997, it might not be affordable in 1998 due to constantly increasing costs for all media.

After test markets are selected there is a choice between two testing methods: (1) Little U.S. Method and (2) As It Falls Method.

The **Little U.S. Method** (a.k.a. Little America) simulates in test market the advertising *pressure* that is generated by the national media plan in the average U.S. market.

This test philosophy assumes the test area is truly representative of the total United States and that results occurring in this area are representative of what will happen nationally.

Table 29.15 shows a national media plan composed of network TV, magazines, and Spot TV in markets that represent 60 percent of U.S. households.

To translate the national plan into test market, the *average* activity is scheduled. For both national media (network TV and magazines), the test market receives the average of the national weight. For Spot TV, the test market receives the average of markets receiving Spot TV and not receiving Spot TV (100 TRPs in 60 percent of the United States plus zero TRPs in 40 percent of the United States for a weighted total of 60 TRPs).

Table 29.15. Alternative Testing Procedures (Total Women TRPs)

		Test Market-Market B	
	National Plan	Little U.S.	As It Falls
Network TV	400	400	380
Magazines	100	100	120
Spot TV (60% U.S.)			
A Markets	150	—	—
B Markets	100	—	100
C Markets	50	—	—
Average	100	60	—
Total		560	600

In the **As It Falls Method** the test markets receive the advertising pressure they normally would receive under the national plan.

Underlying the As It Falls method is the premise that all products have variations in sales potential and test markets should recognize these differences.

With a Little U.S. method, Table 29.15 shows that the test market receives 560 TRPs, simulating the *average* weight delivered in the *average* market. In fact, no market in the U.S. might actually receive this level within the national plan. With the As It Falls method, TRP activity varies according to the local delivery of national media forms, and according to the delivery of the local media forms being used.

Both methods can be used to project national test results. Regardless of which method is employed, most research professionals would advise that more than one test market be used. Ideally, several markets that collectively represent the true average of the national media plan should be included in the test.

Within either testing method it is desirable to schedule local activity that closely resembles the national media being used (Table 29.16). Following are the guidelines for local media use:

- **Television.** Use *cut-ins* whenever possible for network TV. A cut-in is the placement of the test commercial in the test market within the network program. The nationally scheduled commercial is cut-over (replaced) by the test commercial. This technique requires you to have network TV scheduled for the test period. With this method, the viewer in the test market sees what she or he normally would see if the test plan were implemented nationally.

    If cut-ins are not available, Spot TV can be used to simulate the network TV weight. However, there are differences between Spot TV and network TV in terms of audience composition, program type, in-program announcements in network versus some spot announcements being aired between programs and reach/frequency accumulation. It is therefore general practice to compensate for the differences by purchasing more TRPs in Spot TV than would normally be scheduled via network TV.

    Although cable TV is listed in Table 29.16 as a lower priority translation device for network (broadcast) TV and Spot TV, it is important that the cable penetration and coverage area be analyzed before electing to use local cable. Although it varies by market, cable penetration is always less then broadcast pen-

Table 29.16. Local Media Simulation of National Plan Media

National Plan	Priority of Local Media To Be Used
Daytime (broadcast) network TV	1. Cut-ins
	2. Day spot (plus compensation)
	3. Early morning plus early fringe (plus compensation)
	4. Daytime cable TV
Primetime (broadcast) network TV	1. Cut-ins
	2. Prime spot (on network affiliated stations)
	3. Independent station prime spot plus prime access
	4. Early/late fringe (plus compensation)
	5. "Prime" cable TV
Early network news TV	Early news spot TV
Late night network TV	Late fringe spot TV
Spot TV	Spot TV
Network cable TV	Local cable TV
Network radio	Spot radio
Spot radio	Spot radio
Magazines	1. Test market editions
	2. Other "similar" magazines
	3. Newspaper-distributed magazines (supplements)
	4. Newspapers
Newspaper-distributed magazines	Supplements
Newspapers	Newspapers
Out-of-home media	Out-of-home media

etration. The lower the cable penetration level, the higher the percentage of the population in the market who will not be exposed to the test advertising. Additionally, because local cable coverage of systems that allow local insertion is sometimes less than the desired coverage area (e.g., the entire DMA), care must be taken to ensure that most, if not all, of the population is geographically covered. Conceivably, a major distribution outlet for the product being tested could be within a geographic area in which the local system has few or no local insertion availabilities.

- **Radio.** Unlike the differences between network TV and Spot TV, network radio and spot radio are virtually identical in terms of environment, commercial positioning, and reach/frequency accumulation. Therefore, network radio can be directly translated into spot radio. Further, there are no adjustments necessary for translating spot radio in the national plan to spot radio in the test market.

- **Print.** If local editions of the magazines used in the national plan are not available in the selected test markets, other magazines with similar editorial formats should be used. If magazines are not available in the test markets, newspaper supplements can be used as the first alternative, and newspapers as the second alternative.

  Although neither supplements nor newspapers have the same editorial environment or readership pattern as magazines, it is best to use these media rather than using totally unrelated media, or not using any print media at all. It is important, however, to analyze the delivery of the local print vehicles relative to the national print media to ensure that there are not wide variations in coverage.

- **Out-of-Home.** Because out-of-home media are local media forms, all can be translated directly.

30

How To Present Media

The objectives of the media presentation are to:

- Display clearly the direction of the media plan.

- Inform the client of the key ingredients.

- Convince the client that the media plan is the best solution to the marketing problem.

The presentation can take one of many visual forms, and the one used depends on the size of audience, the amount of material to be presented, and the complexity of the material shown. The decision to use one of these forms should be made well in advance of the final preparation of material to ensure that the correct typeface is used and that the amount of material on a given page or chart befits the presentation form.

Through-the-Book

This form of presentation is generally used in smaller, informal meetings. The planner literally walks the client through the media plan, page by page, reading the contents and highlighting the more important aspects. With this form of presentation, the planner can present very complex information and allow the audience to spend as much time as desired on each page. Control is therefore more difficult than with other forms where the planner totally controls the pace of the presentation. It is very important that each page be numbered and that the planner periodically remind the audience which page is being discussed. If you don't do this, you lose the audience—everybody

179

will be on different pages, some well ahead of where you want them to be.

Blowup Charts

This form is more formal than the through-the-book form, but it also is for use only in smaller meetings. The physical size of the charts is generally not large enough to be seen by people sitting more than 10 feet away. The material presented should be less cluttered than with the through-the-book method: Tighter sentences (but never cryptic); more use of bar charts and graphs than actual numbers; less detail.

Transparencies

The use of transparencies with an overhead projector is a compromise between the previous two forms of presentations. It allows you to present more detailed material to a larger audience.

Pad/Blackboard

Unless you are extremely well rehearsed and remember all important points and numbers, and can write quickly and legibly, it's best to prepare these materials in advance of the presentation.

Slides

Slides on a slide projector is the most formal of the presentation forms and can be used for any size audience. It is also the highest quality form and usually expensive to reproduce.

Computer-generated slides are part of electronic systems that tie a computer to a projector (e.g., transparency projector). This method allows large visual display of text and graphs created on a computer. Some systems allow manipulation of text and graphs in real time.

TV Monitor

A TV monitor can be used in several ways, such as with a VCR to play a prerecorded videotape, to display computer-generated text and graphs (when tied to a computer), and to demonstrate research and analytical capabilities through data manipulation in real time.

In presenting media, remember that much of the language is complex and at least one person in the room generally will not be familiar with the jargon of GRPs, reach, frequency, etc. The planner should address this by offering a brief explanation of the terms as they are used.

Presenting Charts

Presenting the numbers on a chart is sometimes more difficult than constructing the chart. The audiences should be walked through all the numbers carefully so they have full appreciation of what is being presented. A good way to present numerical data is to approach it step by step, reading from left to right, from top to bottom. We will use Table 30.1 to illustrate a good approach.

1. Describe the purpose of the chart: This chart shows carbonated soft drink consumption by women by age.

2. Read the column headings across: We display the distribution of population by age, the percentage of each age group who drank soft drinks in the last month, and the percentage of each age group who drank low-calorie cola-type soft drinks in that period.

3. Read the first vertical column: We show this data for each age group: Total women, women aged 18 to 24, 25 to 34, 35 to 44, etc.

Table 30.1. Profile of Adult Women Who Drink Carbonated Soft Drinks

	% Population	Drank Any in Last Month		Drank Low-Calorie Cola in Last Month	
		%	Index	%	Index
Total women	100.0	83.0	100	17.6	100
18–24	17.9	94.4	170	22.1	126
25–34	20.7	90.0	99	21.7	123
35–44	15.5	86.3	85	18.8	107
45–54	15.6	83.4	84	19.9	113
55–64	13.7	78.5	86	12.2	69
65 & older	17.1	63.2	76	9.7	55

Source: Simmons.

4. Read the numerical data vertically: Women aged 18 to 24 represent 17.9 percent of all adult women; women 25 to 34 account for 20.7 percent of the total women population, etc.

5. Read the next column of data, relating it to the first, from top to bottom: Of all adult women, 83 percent drank a soft drink in the last month; 94.4 percent of women aged 18 to 24 drank soft drinks in the last month, and as we move into older age groups, the percentage who drank soft drinks declines.

6. Explain mathematical computations, if any: If we divide the 94.4 percent women in the 18 to 24 age group by the average consumption for all women of 83 percent, we arrive at an index of 170, indicating that the concentration of soft drink drinkers is 70 percent greater among 18-to-24-year-olds than that found in the population as a whole. Note that the index drops as we move through the age groups, showing that as a woman gets older, she is increasingly less likely to be a soft drink consumer.

7. Explain additional material: We have also displayed the percentage of women who drank low-calorie cola-type soft drinks to see if it has a different profile. It does. Note that the index is above 100 for women in the four age groups from 18 to 54, indicating that the low-calorie drinker tends to be slightly older in profile than the average soft drink consumer.

Regardless of the data you present, or the makeup of the audience, you must be totally familiar with the material. To achieve that familiarity, you must rehearse time and time again.

Because much of media planning involves numbers, a media presentation will often cite numerical analyses and findings. This could become boring and tiresome for the audience. Keep as much ambient lighting on in the room as possible. Darkness and snoozing sometime go hand in hand. Periodically reprise an agenda (table of contents) so the audience knows how much longer it has to remain seated and attentive. Use colorful bar graphs and pie charts to replace detailed spreadsheets (witness, for example, how boring the previous table is).

Generally, the media planner should present the media plan to the client. Aside from pride of authorship, the planner is the expert, knowing more about media than anyone else in the room. The intricacies of the construction, as well as intimate knowledge of the components, argue that the planner should make the presentation, both to explain and to field any questions/problems that might arise at the presentation.

Keep in mind that the objectives of the presentation are to inform, convince, and get approval.

31

Negotiating a Media Buy

Media time and space are commodities. Blank pages in magazines and newspapers, air time within TV and radio programs, and poster space are sold and bought. The costs of these commodities is negotiable, as are the specific placement of the advertising message within the media vehicle, and the ancillary items that might be part of the overall buy. The techniques used for an effective negotiation are similar (in concept if not in specifics) to those used for all negotiations. How well you negotiate a buy has much to do with negotiating skills, which are learned over time and as a result of going through many negotiations, as well as being taught by skillful negotiators. Skills involve your demeanor during the negotiation, when to offer and counteroffer, how to listen, how to speak, what to say, and so forth. There are books and seminars on the art of negotiation, which could prove helpful for any buyer—junior or senior. Notwithstanding that skills must be developed to become an effective media buyer, some components of the media negotiation process can be (and should be) learned before even the first buy is made.

Knowing media dynamics is obviously critically important. If buying TV or radio, you must know the dynamics of rating, PUT, share, CPP, etc.; if buying print media: RPC, in-home/out-of-home, CPM, audience accumulation, etc.; if buying out-of-home media: showing, DEC, etc. No person charged with spending an advertiser's media budget should enter into buying negotiations without full knowledge of media dynamics and analysis techniques. For example, if a new TV program or magazine is being purchased, it is important to understand how audience delivery might be predicted because a bad prediction will automatically lead to an inefficient and possibly ineffective buy.

The Objective of the Buy

The objective of a media buy is never to "buy 100 TRPs" or "schedule an insertion." The objective always deals with delivering a specific creative message that will have a positive impact on consumers and motivate them to do something: buy a product or service, go to a store, etc. A media buyer should never get so involved with the trees that he or she loses sight of the forest. Knowing the objective of the buy is of paramount importance. For example, if the objective is to produce a high level of reach within a relatively short period of time, it would be counterproductive to negotiate for many spots on a few programs (because they might be cost-efficient) and not buy fewer spots on each of many high-rated programs (because they happen to be less cost-efficient).

Marketplace Conditions

In various sections of this book we used the cost of media to demonstrate the dynamics of certain terms (e.g., CPM, CPP), and to give examples of how to analyze different media vehicles and alternative media plans. All of the costs are hypothetical. None are from *rate cards*. Although many media vendors publish rate cards, the rates in these cards, with rare exception, are not used by either the media salesperson or the media buyer. For the most part, media costs are totally negotiable.

Never assume that the costs paid yesterday will be the same today. Costs vary among media forms and for the components within a form, primarily as a result of supply and demand: how much commercial inventory is available (which, with the possible exception of print media, is a relative constant) and how many media buyers want to buy that inventory. The overall level of demand fluctuates throughout the year, and from year to year, based on many factors. For example, there's usually more demand during a generally healthy, growing economy, and in the weeks preceding major holidays (e.g., Independence Day, Christmas), governmental elections, and back-to-school. Demand also varies from one geographic market to another. The factors affecting local demand are exacerbated by local phenomenon, such as how many local advertisers are in the marketplace buying TV, radio, or outdoor. Lastly, demand levels vary among specific TV programs or radio stations based on the medium's audience delivery performance. There is usually more demand for *hot* (high-rated) programs or stations.

Because supply/demand fluctuates, the media buyer can be in the driver's seat if he or she has a good sense of marketplace conditions, i.e., knowing if it is a buyer's or seller's market. There are several ways to know this:

1. By having a continuous history of buying the medium, the buyer can analyze trends.

2. By negotiating with all of the media suppliers' sales representatives (e.g., all the TV stations' sales representatives in Market X), the buyer can establish a consensus.

3. By knowing the overall trends of a media form (e.g., by reading advertising industry trade journals), the buyer can get a pulse on how strong or weak the medium is.

Supplier's Cost versus Buyer's Offer

A media supplier incurs costs for providing its medium to advertisers. Costs include, for example, the actual production of the TV or radio program, newspaper or magazine; the distribution of the medium to the consumer (e.g., transmission equipment, postage); and staff salaries, benefits, and general overhead. The supplier strives to generate advertising sales revenues that exceed costs, i.e., make a profit. Although no media supplier is (as is no businessperson) adverse to making as much profit as possible, it's financially foolhardy to bear a loss.

Although it is very difficult for the media supplier to assess the actual cost for a specific commercial unit or print ad, the supplier has a good idea of the approximate price an advertiser should pay to cover the costs and effect a profit for the medium. The price offered by a media salesperson is what he or she believes the advertising unit is worth. The actual worth of the unit is based on what the buyer is willing to pay. Just as retail outlets can sell certain items for cost or below cost because they are making profits on the remaining merchandise they offer for sale, so can media suppliers sell certain programs/pages/units at break-even or at a small loss. The amount of inventory that is sold at a loss ties back to supply and demand. Always, however, if demand is high, there is no inventory sold below cost.

No media salesperson will quarrel with a media buyer who is willing to pay the *offered* price. There will be disagreement, however, if the buyer's offer is less than what the media supplier believes should be paid, and possible disengagement from the negotiation if the buyer's price offer is less than the media supplier's cost. The media buyer certainly wants the best possible media buy at the lowest possible price, but the seller cannot always sell a program or package below cost.

Both buyer and seller are trying to get the best deal. There might always be an opportunity to lower costs "just a little bit more" than you or the seller might find realistic, but doing this could produce ill feelings and resentments. This will unquestionably rebound in the long run. For example, when last-minute opportunities become available, a media salesperson will instinctively first call those buyers who he or she considered "fair" during the previous negotiations, and might totally avoid calling the buyer who attempted to inequitably grind down costs.

Added Value

Many media buys can be enhanced with relatively little or no increase in spending. These enhancements are known by many names, but mostly as *merchandising* or *added value*. The following is a sample of the many enhancements buyers can seek:

- On-air mentions from a radio DJ during a station contest/give-away.

- Opening or closing *billboards* stating things like "this program brought to you by . . . ."

- Tickets to a sporting event might be available from a TV station that, for example, has bartered airtime for tickets with a sports team.

- Distribution of a magazine issue, with a cover letter from the publisher, to the advertiser's preselected list of recipients.

- An advertisement in a cable operator's local cable listings magazine sent to the system's subscribers.

- A remote broadcast conducted by a radio station at the location of a new store opening.

- Inclusion in a special issue of a periodical when you have purchased the standard issue.

These added-value enhancements should not, however, compromise the primary intent of the buy, which is always to deliver a specific creative message to media audiences. Nor should these enhancements compromise the cost-efficiency of the buy. For example, a radio station that might not make the cut on a media buy (because of cost, cost-efficiency, audience composition, etc.) should not be included in the buy just because the station is willing to promote the advertised product on its call-in game show. On the other hand, merchandising offers could be used as a tiebreaker when deciding between identical or very similar media delivery alternatives.

The added value received as part of the buy should always reflect the objective of the buy and the creative effort. Media delivery and merchandising must be integrated so the consumer receives one coordinated communication. Consumers do not distinguish, per se, between paid advertising and merchandising. For example, if the objective of the buy is to introduce a new product for a fast food restaurant, a merchandising effort that distributes free meal coupons for *any* product should not be considered an appropriate enhancement.

It is always best to negotiate for added value during the buying process, not after a buy has been negotiated. If merchandising is part of the original buy negotiations, the added-value effort stands a better chance of reflecting the objective of the buy—because the buyer and seller are embroiled in trying to achieve the objective. It is also human nature that the seller will work harder at providing added-value enhancements during the buy negotiations than after a media buy has been put to bed.

Monitoring

A media buy is not finished after it is bought. A buy only provides an intent. The intent is that a creative message will be carried by the medium: in certain TV programs, in particular radio dayparts, in specific magazine issues, in agreed sections of a newspaper, etc. Any number of things could prevent fulfillment, such as the videotape/cassette of the commercial not arriving at the station on time, a commercial preemption due to a news bulletin, a station mislogging a spot, or a printing error resulting in your ad being backed by an advertisement with an on-page/tear-out coupon.

Involvement in the buy, and monitoring the buy as it progresses (i.e., as it is on-air or running in print media) provides a degree of assurance that the objective of the buy is being fulfilled—that the creative message is being exposed to media audiences. If spots are missed or ads misrun, *makegoods* should immediately be negotiated (or cash credits taken if the available makegood is unacceptable). With long-term broadcast buys (i.e., a continuous campaign or extended flights) rating performance should be monitored to the extent that rating reports are available. If performance on the purchased programs/stations is downtrending, immediate action should be taken to make up any perceived loss in media delivery.

Postanalysis

Every media buy is negotiated for media delivery that will happen in the future. As such, the buyer is predicting media performance: how many TRPs will be delivered, how much circulation will a magazine issue have. For example, if a buyer is making a buy in September for a TV schedule that will air in November, the buyer has only historical rating information on which to base predictions of future rating delivery. As solid as the predictions might appear to be, actual performance (in November) could vary from what was predicted.

The buyer must do a postanalysis: analyzing performance based on the reported media delivery for the period in which the buy ran. For example, a November buy for TV should be postanalyzed using the November Nielsen TV rating report; for November radio, the Fall Arbitron radio ratings report; for a November print ad, the six month ABC circulation statement listing November's circulation. The analysis should report the media delivery for the segment in which the creative message was delivered. If a TV commercial aired on Tuesday at 9:10 P.M. in Program X, the rating for the 9:00–9:15 P.M. quarter-hour should be used. Using broad averages, such as 9:00–10:00 P.M., or primetime, or Sunday–Saturday, misreports what actually was delivered. If *performance guarantees* were built into the buy during the initial negotiation (e.g., the buyer and seller agreed a package of spots would deliver 100 TRPs), and the postanalysis reveals underdelivery relative to the goal, the buyer should negotiate for bonus (gratis) delivery at a later date to make up for the underdelivery.

One Last Thought

Because a media negotiation involves money, and because there is always pressure on the buyer and the seller to effect the best possible deal for their respective companies, tension and possibly stress could ensue. Further, the control of the money is always in the buyer's hands, which could lead to an exaggerated sense of power. All these factors could affect emotions and instigate hostility at the negotiating table.

A buyer can be tough and fair, and be respected by the seller. The seller, in turn, will work hard at being fair and helping the buyer accomplish the objective of the buy. Conversely, a rude buyer might not receive the seller's full cooperation during the negotiation and conceivably during the monitoring of the buy. Always keep in mind the human aspects as well as the business aspects.

32

Principles of Media Management

Numbers don't think . . . people do.

Sound research and thorough investigation, combined with intelligence and logic, are mandatory before astute media decisions can be made. But too often these decisions are based on numbers alone.

Numbers are a big part of the media planner's and media buyer's life. They are used to analyze alternatives, provide direction, and eventually help make a decision. Too often, however, the numbers are used as a crutch—as the primary rationale for selecting one medium over another or one television spot rather than another. They are often viewed myopically. All that goes into generating the numbers, all the varying research techniques used, and all the pitfalls and dangers surrounding the numbers are blurred.

The computer has been a windfall, almost a necessity. A myriad of numbers can be fed in, and the computer can be programmed to spit out an equally mind-boggling list; a list fashioned to any number of needs and displayed with clarity in order to allow one to simply run one's fingers down the columns to choose the best answer. The advances in sophisticated decisions in a more competitive climate, in turn, argue for use of the computer to deal with the multiple machinations.

Media planning is now a sophisticated art managed along scientific principles. It is an integral part of every marketing plan. There are now more media outlets than ever, with more complicated research to prove one superior to the other. Costs for media tend to increase each year, making investment decisions even more critical. The broadcast marketplace is extremely volatile, causing buyers to constantly monitor pricing and programming. No easy task.

Something could easily get lost. Sometimes the quantity of numbers generated prevents planners and buyers from spending the time to look into the numbers and see what made them happen in the first place. Sometimes the numbers become the rationale rather than the guideline. Sometimes the human element is lost, and creative thinking is subjugated to an almost nonexistent role. And that is a pity.

What should we media planners do? Here are ten guidelines:

1. **Be a money manager.**

   The client has entrusted you with his or her money to make the *best* media decisions. Your recommendations become an investment—and the client is looking for the greatest return-on-investment. Never forget that the numbers in a media plan are backed with real dollars.

2. **Remember, effectiveness is primary.**

   Effectiveness, and not necessarily efficiency, is the key criterion. Go beyond the numbers in making recommendations that will deliver more effective advertising. Have the guts to defend your opinions. Appreciate that all the numbers are *estimates,* based on a sampling of the population. They can swing up or down depending on the research technique, the time of year, and the particular sample chosen. All the numbers have statistical tolerance, a leeway for variation that can be expected from the average number shown. Decisions based on a 10-cent difference in a cost-per-thousand, or a 2 percent advantage of one plan over another, are shaky. In the real world, the exact opposite might be true.

3. **Be creative.**

   The media function does not exist in a vacuum. It must be planned and implemented as an extension of marketing and creative needs. Every media action must have a marketing rationale. The media planner has an obligation to be creative, just as much as do other areas of an advertising agency. The creative idea can be big and expensive, but more often it is little more than a better way of doing the usual. Think. Innovate. Create.

4. **Be conversant with all media forms.**

   Specializing in one medium, to the exclusion of all others, breeds narrow thinking. Read all trade journals and textbooks available. Attend seminars, speeches, and conventions related to media. Rub elbows with fellow planners and buyers, and media salespeople, to keep on top of the latest developments. You'll become more rounded in your profession and thereby make a more significant contribution.

5. **Evaluate all reasonable alternatives.**

   This is hard work, and it takes time. But to make hasty recommendations for the sake of expedience can result in a lackluster, ineffective plan and execution. Use the computer's capabilities.

6. **Be involved in the total marketing picture.**

   A media plan is an extension of the marketing plan and should reflect the marketing objectives and creative strategy. Media planning and buying cannot exist in a vacuum and be effective. Involvement with the account and creative groups, as well as with the client and his product, is mandatory.

7. **Maintain what you have built.**

   Maintenance is as important as building. The media plan that is executed does not always perform as anticipated. Significant losses in delivery and effectiveness can result if a television spot is missed or reproduction in a magazine is poor. Take the time to monitor performance. Upgrade when possible and correct discrepancies immediately.

8. **Keep everyone informed.**

   You are the expert in media and charged with devising and executing media plans with sound rationale. Your job becomes easier and more productive if the account groups, creative groups, the client, and your fellow media colleagues know what is happening in the total media scene. Dissemination of information argues for a discipline of thinking and begets better media recommendations. Shower your clients with information.

9. **Establish rapport with media suppliers.**

   Media salespeople often know more about their specific medium than you do. They can be a storehouse of pertinent information that will help your media decisions. Let them into your office, return their phone calls. Be candid in your dealings with them and let them know your needs in order to have fruitful meetings that can benefit the client in the long run.

10. **Contribute beyond media.**

You are an advertising person who happens to be expert in media. Your greatest contribution to the client will be in your specialty, but this should not inhibit you from recommending marketing, creative, or new product ideas that can build the client's business.

Glossary

Added value—Additional media delivery, merchandising or promotion provided to an advertiser by a purchased medium, often gratis, that adds greater "value" to the media buy

Addressable—The ability of media such as magazines and TV to direct advertising to specific individuals

Adjacency—A program or time period that is scheduled immediately preceding or following a scheduled program on the same station. Also called **Break position**

Affiliate—A broadcast station bound to a contractual relationship with one or more networks to carry network-originated programs and announcements

Agate line—A newspaper space measurement that measures one column wide and $1/14$ inch deep

A.M. (amplitude modulation)—The transmission of sound in radio broadcasting in which the amplitude (power) of a transmitting wave is modulated (changed) to simulate the original sound

Announcement—An advertising message in broadcast media. Announcements generally are of 60-, 30-, 20-, or 10-second duration. Synonymous with "commercial"

Area of Dominant Influence (ADI)—See **TV market**

As it falls—A method for simulating media plans in test markets

Audience composition—The percentage of individuals in each demographic cell

Audimeter—An electronic device attached to TV sets in sample households of A. C. Nielsen. It records set usage and channel tuned on a minute-by-minute basis

Audit Bureau of Circulation (ABC)—An organization formed by media, advertisers, and advertising agencies to audit the circulation statements of its member magazines and newspapers

Availability—The commercial position in a program or between programs on a given station or network that is available for purchase by an advertiser. "Avails" for short

Average audience—In broadcast, the number of homes (or individuals) tuned to the average minute of a program. In print media, the number of individuals who looked into an average issue of a publication

Barter—The acquisition of quantities of commercial time from broadcast stations in exchange for merchandise

Basic cable—The subscription to a cable system that allows the household to receive all broadcast and cable origination programming that is not otherwise sold at higher rates. See **Pay per view**

Billboard—In broadcast, free airtime given to a sponsoring advertiser. In outdoor media, an advertising structure

Black & white page—An advertising page that uses no color. Abbreviated as P B/W

Bleed—In print media, to extend the illustration or copy to the edge of a page so there is no white border. In outdoor, a poster panel that uses the entire available space

Brand development index (BDI)—A numerical display indicating the geographic or demographic areas of a product's strength or weakness

Break position—A commercial aired between programs as opposed to within a program. Also called **Adjacency**

Broadcast coverage area—The geographic area within which a signal from an originating television station can be received

Busorama—An advertising unit within transit media

Cable system—A company that receives via satellite and airwaves television programming (and commercials) and retransmits to subscribing households within a defined geographic area

Cable TV (CATV)—A communications system that provides special lines rented by a firm to a household either to bring in outside television stations with a clear picture, and/or provide special programming on a direct hookup

Car card—An advertising unit within transit media

Cash discount—A discount granted by the media to an advertiser for prompt payment, usually 2 percent of the net amount

Category Development Index (CDI)—The same as a brand development index, but using product category sales rather than product sales

Chain break—The time between network programs when a network affiliated station identifies itself

Circulation—In print media, the number of copies sold or distributed by a publication. In broadcast, the number of homes owning a set within a station's coverage area. In outdoor, the number of people passing an advertisement who have an opportunity to view it

Clearance—The broadcast stations carrying a network or syndicated program

Clock spectacular—An advertising unit within transit media

Closing date—The date set by a publication for receipt of material for an advertisement to appear in a forthcoming issue

Clusters—The grouping of population groups into unique demographic/ psychographic segments for purposes of description and analysis of product and media consumption patterns

Combination rate—A special rate for advertisers using more than one vehicle in a group of publications

Consolidated Metropolitan Statistical Area (CMSA)—Made up of component PMSAs

Continuity discount—A rate discount allowed an advertiser who purchases a specific schedule within a series of a publication's issues

Controlled circulation—The circulation of a publication that is sent free and addressed to specified individuals

Cost-per-point (CPP)—The unit cost (e.g., a 30-second commercial) divided by the rating of the program in which the commercial will appear

Cost-per-thousand (CPM)—The cost per 1,000 individuals (or homes) delivered by a medium or media schedule

County size—Designation of a county into one of four categories as defined by A. C. Nielsen based on population

Coupons—A trade- or consumer-oriented promotion providing an incentive that accelerates the purchase decision.

Coverage—The percentage of persons (or homes) covered by a medium

Cut-in—The insertion of a commercial, at the local level, into a network program

Daily effective circulation (DEC)—The number of people who pass an out-of-home display (e.g., poster) during the average day

Dayparts—Times of broadcast for television and radio

Daytime—In TV, the daytime hours of programming, usually 10 A.M. to 4:30 P.M. EST. In radio, generally 10 A.M. to 3 P.M.

Delayed broadcast (DB)—The term given to a network TV program that is delayed for airing at a different time in a given market

Demographic editions—Special editions of magazines directed to specific audience types

Designated Market Area (DMA)—See **TV market**

Direct broadcast satellite (DBS)—Reception of TV/Radio signals directly from a satellite via a "personal" satellite dish owned/leased by an individual household. Dishes are of various sizes with the smallest being approximately 18 inches in diameter

Dispersion—The level of scattering of commercials or ads across programs or print vehicles, e.g., high dispersion indicates the use of many different programs/magazines

Drive time—The morning and afternoon hours of radio broadcasting; morning drive: 6 to 10 A.M.; afternoon drive: 3 to 7 P.M.

Duplication—The number of individuals (or homes) exposed to more than one advertising message through a media schedule

Effective reach—The number of individuals (or homes) reached by a media schedule at a given level of frequency

Efficiency—The relationship of media cost to audience delivery. See **Cost-per-thousand**

Exposure—A person's physical contact (visual and/or audio) with an advertising medium or message

Fiber-optic cable—Composed of pure glass strands able to transmit significantly more information (video/audio/text) than conventional cable or phone lines

Fixed position—In broadcast, a commercial unit purchased with nonpreemption guarantees. In print, a position guaranteed to the advertiser in specified issues.

Flat rate—The nondiscountable rate charged by a newspaper for advertising

Flighting—Scheduling a heavy advertising effort for a period of time, followed by a hiatus, then coming back with another schedule at the same or a higher or lower level

Format—General reference is to the type of programming broadcast by a radio station (e.g., rock, classical, etc.)

Four-color page—An advertising page that utilizes three colors as well as black. Abbreviated as P4C or 4-CP

Franchise position—A valued position because of editorial adjacency, program value, or geographical location

Frequency—The number of times individuals (or homes) are exposed to an advertising message

Frequency discount—A rate discount allowed an advertiser who purchases a specific schedule within a specified period of time

Frequency distribution—The array of reach according to the level of frequency delivered to each group

F.M. (Frequency modulation)—A clear radio signal, without static or fading, that results from the adjustment of the frequency of the transmitting wave to the originating sound

Fringe time—In TV, the evening hours that precede and follow primetime, usually 4:30–7:30 P.M. and 11 P.M.–1 A.M. EST

Gatefold—A folded advertising page that, unfolded, is bigger in dimension than the regular page

Gross Rating Points (GRPs)—The sum of ratings delivered by a given list of media vehicles

Hiatus—A period of nonactivity

Homes Using TV (HUT)—The percentage of homes using TV at a given time

Identification (ID)—In broadcast, a commercial that is no more than 10 seconds long (visual) and 8 seconds long (audio)

Impressions—The sum of all exposures

Independent station—A broadcast station not affiliated with a "line" network

Index—A percentage that relates numbers to a base

Information superhighway—The integration of television, radio, computers, telephones, fax machines, etc., which, combined with other technological advances, such as fiber optics and digital compression, is changing the transmission and reception of video, audio, and data

In-home readers—Those people reading a magazine in their own home

Interactive media—Media forms (e.g., TV and personal computers) that allow the consumer to electronically manipulate and/or respond to video/audio/text being transmitted to the consumer

Interconnect—Cable systems joined electronically or otherwise for the purpose of selling advertising to reach larger population groups than represented by any one system

Issue life—The length of time it takes a magazine to be read by the maximum measurable audience

Junior panel—A scaled-down version of a 30-sheet poster

Lead-in (lead-out)—Program preceding (or following) the time period or program being analyzed
Line networks—TV signals transmitted over telephone lines from one station to the next, or transmitted simultaneously to all stations via satellite
Little U.S.—A method for simulating media plans in test markets

Makegood—In broadcast, a commercial position given in lieu of the announcement missed due to the fault of the station or network. In print, the free repeat of an advertisement to compensate for the publication's error in the original insertion
Media mix—The use of two or more media different media forms in one plan.
Merchandising—Promotional activities that complement advertising and that are provided free or at a nominal charge by media purchased for advertising
Metro area—Also MSA

Near Video On Demand (NVOD)—Capability of receiving movies or other programming fare via cable TV or DBS near the time a consumer wishes to view program, e.g., within 15 minutes of the desired time
Newspaper Designated Market—The geographic area in which the publisher believes the newspaper has its greatest strength

O & Os—The stations owned and operated by the broadcast networks
Objectives, media—The statement of action required of media to fulfill marketing needs
Off-network programs—TV programs that aired on network TV that are replaying via syndication
One sheet—An outdoor advertisement usually measuring 12 feet by 4 feet
Only only both—A display of audience reach for those receiving only medium A, only medium B, and both A and B
Open rate—The maximum rate charged by a magazine—its rate for one insertion
Outdoor—Media placed out of doors
Out-of-home readers—Those people reading a magazine outside of their own homes

Painted bulletin—An outdoor advertising structure on which advertising is painted directly
Passalong readers—Readers of a publication that they or other members of their household did not purchase
Pay Per View (PPV)—The payment to a cable operator for the reception of a specific program (e.g., movie, sports event)
Penetration—The proportion of persons (or homes) that are physically able to be exposed to a medium

People Using Radio (PUR)—The percentage of people using radio at a given time

People Using TV (PUT)—The percentage of people using TV at a given time

Permanent paints—An outdoor bulletin at a specific location that is not rotated to other locations

Point-of-purchase display—An advertising display at the place where consumers purchase goods or services (e.g., counter card at a retail outlet)

Porta-panel—A mobile poster panel that is wheeled to a given location (e.g., a supermarket parking lot)

Poster-panel—An outdoor advertising structure on which a preprinted advertisement is displayed

Preemption—The displacement of a regularly scheduled program, or announcement, on a broadcast facility by the station or network

Preferred position—Print advertisements scheduled in specific positions as agreed by the advertiser and the publication (opposite of ROP)

Preprinted insert—An advertisement printed by the advertiser and supplied to a publication in which it is inserted for distribution to media audiences

Primary Metropolitan Statistical Area (PMSA)—Made up of one or more MSAs

Primary readers—Readers who purchased a magazine or are members in a household where the publication was purchased

Prime access—The half-hour immediately preceding primetime television in which local stations were originally charged by the Federal Communications Commission to broadcast programs in the interest of the local community

Primetime—In TV, usually a three-hour time period (Monday–Saturday) and three-and-a-half-hour time period (Sunday) designated by a station as its highest viewing time. Usually 8–11 P.M. (Monday–Saturday) and 7:30–11 P.M. (Sunday) EST. In radio, generally 6–10 A.M. and 3–7 P.M.

Psychographics—A term identifying personality characteristics and attitudes that affect a person's lifestyle and purchasing behavior

Pulsing—A flighting technique that calls for a continuous base of support augmented by intermittent bursts of heavy pressure

Quintile distribution—A display of frequency among audiences grouped into equal fifths of total reach

Radio daypart—Time periods in a 24-hour day during which radio programs are broadcast

Random combination—A mathematical formula for obtaining audience reach for two or more media forms

Rate base—The circulation of a print vehicle upon which advertising space rates are based; it may or may not be guaranteed by the publication

Rate card—A pamphlet, brochure, or single sheet of paper that states the costs for advertising on or in an advertising vehicle as well as other pertinent information relating to the vehicle, e.g., circulation, mechanical requirements, etc.

Rate holder—A unit of space or time, usually small, that is used to maintain or establish a contractual agreement over a period of time

Rating—The percentage of individuals (or homes) exposed to a particular TV or radio program

Reach—The number of different individuals (or homes) exposed to a media schedule within a given period of time

Readers per copy—The number of individuals reading a given issue of a publication

Rebate—A payment to the advertiser by a medium when the advertising schedule exceeds the contractual commitments originally agreed to and the advertisement earns a lower rate

Retail Trading Zone—A geographic area around a central city

Rollout—A marketing procedure where advertising is expanded into progressively more areas over time

ROP—Run-of-Press. A position request to run an advertisement anywhere in the publication

Rotary display—The purchase of painted bulletins whereby the display face is periodically rotated to new locations

Scatter—Purchasing announcements in broadcast in many different programs

Sets in use—Antiquated and replaced by **Homes Using TV.** Referred to the number of sets turned on at a given time

Share—The percentage of Homes Using TV (or radio) tuned to a particular program

Short rate—In print media, the dollar penalty an advertiser pays for not fulfilling space requirements that were contracted for at the beginning of a given period, usually one year. The penalty is the difference in rate between the contracted rate and the actual earned rate.

Showing—Gross rating points within outdoor advertising. The number of posters displayed on different vehicles within transit media

Simulcast—The concurrent broadcasting of a television or radio program

Single copy (sales)—Copies of a magazine or newspaper that are sold at newsstands, etc., as opposed to by subscription

SMSA—Standard Metropolitan Statistical Area (p. 68)

Special—Broadcast program that is not a part of the usual programming offered by a station or network

Split run—A scheduling technique whereby two different pieces of copy are run in the circulation of a publication with no one reader receiving both advertisements

Sponsorship—The purchase of more than one announcement within a program allowing advertisers to receive bonus time via billboards

Spots—Refers to TV commercial announcements, e.g., 30-second commercials

Spot TV or radio—Purchase of time on a non-network, nonsyndication basis

Strategies, Media—The media solution used to fulfill the media objectives

Supplements—Newspaper-distributed magazines

Survey area—See **Total survey area**

Syndication—A method of placing a program on a market-by-market basis

Tabloid—A newspaper smaller than the size of standard newspaper, such as the *New York Daily News*

Target rating points (TRPs)—The sum of ratings delivered by a given list of media vehicles

Television daypart—Time periods in a 24-hour day in which TV programs are broadcast

30 sheets—Synonymous with posters

Three Hits (3+)—An "effective reach" theory and term. The term indicates the amount of reach obtained among audiences exposed to three or more advertising messages

Tolerance—The range of error, plus or minus the reported number, in audience research for any medium

Total Survey Area—In radio, the area in which radio signals from an originating market can be received

Transit—Advertising placed on public transportation sites and vehicles

TV market—An unduplicated television area to which a county is assigned on the basis of highest share of viewing

UHF (ultra high frequency)—The band added to the VHF band for television transmission—channels 14–83

Unwired networks—A combination of TV or radio stations in separate markets cooperating to sell advertising at a discounted rate, generally through the national sales organization representing all the stations

VHF (very high frequency)—TV channels 2–13

Video on demand (VOD)—Capability of receiving movies or other programming fare via cable TV or DBS at exactly the time a consumer wishes to view the program

Viewers per viewing household (VPVH)—The number of people viewing or listening to a program in each viewing home

Webs (obsolete)—Referred to what is now known as TV networks

Weighted average—The arithmetic average obtained by adding the products of numbers "weighted" by a predetermined value

Index

About the Author

Upon graduation from high school in 1959, Jim Surmanek got a job in the mailroom at *Parade* magazine. He eventually became *Parade*'s associate research director. He was hired by Ogilvy & Mather/New York in 1966 to help run its media research operation and later took on responsibilities in the Spot TV buying and media planning departments. For part of his tenure in New York he detoured from his media career to run the Avon business as account supervisor.

When O&M opened its Chicago office in 1976, Jim was asked to establish and build its media department. During his five years in Chicago he became a senior vice president and a member of O&M/US Management Council.

He journeyed to Mexico City in 1981 as marketing director on special assignment and soon after went to Los Angeles to be O&M's executive media director. He was later named general manager of the office, overseeing media, research, finance, account management, human resources, and new business.

He left O&M in 1986 and joined J. Walter Thompson/Los Angeles as senior vice president, executive media director. While at JWT he also established and ran its Direct Response Division to service the agency's then largest client. In 1988 he accepted a position with McCann-Erickson/Los Angeles as senior vice-president where he was management supervisor on Sony Pictures Entertainment, as well as serving as director of new business development for the agency's office, and as executive media director.

In 1992, Jim joined International Communications Group, Inc.—one of the largest independent media planning and buying companies in the United States—as senior vice-president, director of client services. In 1994, Jim returned to Chicago to open a new office for ICG where he serves as general manager.

TITLES OF INTEREST IN
PRINT AND BROADCAST MEDIA

ESSENTIALS OF MEDIA PLANNING, by Arnold M. Barban, Steven M. Cristol, and Frank J. Kopec

STRATEGIC MEDIA PLANNING, by Kent M. Lancaster and Helen E. Katz

MEDIA MATH, by Robert W. Hall

INTRODUCTION TO ADVERTISING MEDIA, by Jim Surmanek

MEDIA PLANNING, by Jim Surmanek

ADVERTISING MEDIA PLANNING, by Jack Sissors and Lincoln Bumba

ADVERTISING MEDIA SOURCEBOOK, by Arnold M. Barban, Donald W. Jugenheimer, and Peter B. Turk

THE FUTURE OF TELEVISION, by Marc Doyle

HOW TO PRODUCE EFFECTIVE TV COMMERCIALS, by Hooper White

HOW TO CREATE EFFECTIVE TV COMMERCIALS, by Huntley Baldwin

THE RADIO AND TELEVISION COMMERCIAL, by Albert C. Book, Norman D. Cary, and Stanley Tannenbaum

DICTIONARY OF BROADCAST COMMUNICATIONS, by Lincoln Diamant

CHILDREN'S TELEVISION, by Cy Schneider

FUNDAMENTALS OF COPY & LAYOUT, by Albert C. Book and C. Dennis Schick

CREATING AND DELIVERING WINNING ADVERTISING AND MARKETING PRESENTATIONS, by Sandra Moriarty and Tom Duncan

HOW TO WRITE A SUCCESSFUL ADVERTISING PLAN, by James W. Taylor

ADVERTISING COPYWRITING, by Philip Ward Burton

STRATEGIC ADVERTISING CAMPAIGNS, by Don E. Schultz

WRITING FOR THE MEDIA, by Sandra Pesmen

THE ADVERTISING PORTFOLIO, by Ann Marie Barry

PUBLIC RELATIONS IN THE MARKETING MIX, by Jordan Goldman

HANDBOOK FOR BUSINESS WRITING, by L. Sue Baugh, Maridell Fryar, and David A. Thomas

HANDBOOK FOR PUBLIC RELATIONS WRITING, by Thomas Bivins

HANDBOOK FOR MEMO WRITING, by L. Sue Baugh

HANDBOOK FOR PROOFREADING, by Laura Anderson

HANDBOOK FOR TECHNICAL WRITING, by James Shelton

UPI STYLEBOOK, by United Press International

FUNDAMENTALS OF SUCCESSFUL NEWSLETTERS, by Thomas Bivins

BUSINESS MAGAZINE PUBLISHING, by Sal Marino

THE PUBLICITY HANDBOOK, by David R. Yale

NTC'S MASS MEDIA DICTIONARY, by R. Terry Ellmore

NTC'S DICTIONARY OF ADVERTISING, by Jack Wiechmann

DICTIONARY OF BROADCAST COMMUNICATIONS, by Lincoln Diamant

HOW TO PRODUCE CREATIVE ADVERTISING, by Ann Keding and Thomas Bivins

HOW TO PRODUCE CREATIVE PUBLICATIONS, by Thomas Bivins and William E. Ryan

5087

For further information or a current catalog, write:
NTC Business Books
a division of NTC *Publishing Group*
4255 West Touhy Avenue
Lincolnwood, Illinois 60646–1975